MODERN CORPORATE ACCOUNTING

Dr. T. F. Kipilimba

Phd. Financial Management

Richmond University. Uk.

PREFACE

Introduction.

The scope of Corporate Accounting was confined to rise day after another after globalization come into practice. A rise in a number of transactions after the bodies' establishment like the European Union, EU, ECOWAS, East African Community etc. but little significance put to the analytical thinking in modern Corporate Accounting system in order to cater all Accounting problems.

Therefore it came within my mind that an accounting textbook is essentially been ranged in order to match with the present raise in number of transactions and modern Corporate accounting styles.

Sources of information are lectures from my professors, from lower level to the highest level, both from tuition, out of tuitions and materials from my lectures academic institutions.

OBJECTIVES OF THE BOOK

1. To show that the subject of Accounting is simple to understand, relevant in practice and interesting to learn.
2. To help both accountants and managers to appreciate the logics of keeping proper records for today and future use.
3. To explain the concepts and accounting theories and practices in a simple way so as readers can group them easily and be able to practice.
4. To provide a book that has a comprehensive coverage for all categories of students.
5. To issue a book that is unique by its nature to other accounting book.

Features of the book

Modern corporate Accounting aims to assist the readers to develop a through understanding of the concepts, theories and practices underlying Accounting in a systematic way. To accomplish this purpose the recent thinking in the field of Accounting has been presented in a most simple and unambiguous and precise manner.

The book contains a comprehensive treatment of topics on:-

The book has stressed the analytical approach for solving accounting problems. Concepts are made simple and clear with simple language if contains well life. The main features of this book are summarized as follows:-

1. Contribution in filling the gape found from various accounting studying manuals.
2. Stimulating students in thinking about the modern accounting techniques, putting into consideration to great technological changes.

ACKNOWLEDGEMENTS

A large number of individuals have contributed in creating this book modern accounting. I am thankful to all of them for their help and encouragement.

Like most textbooks, this book has drawn from the works of a large number of researchers and authors in a field of accounting and finance.

A number of standard and popular textbooks in the fields has also influenced my writing this book.

I express my gratitude to all of them. A number of problems, illustrations and exercises have been drawn from based on examinations of different universities in different countries as well as international professional bodies from UK, Tanzania (worldwide) such as ACCA, NBAA, CIMA etc.

I have drawn materials from different corners. However, there might be some unintended errors. I shall feel obliged if they will be brought to my notice.

I express my gratitude to all profession multitudes worldwide for their contributions or for making suggestion for the improvement of the book or extending their support and encouragement.

I could not mention the names of friends who have been a source of motivation to me, because it is a very long list. Nevertheless, I thank you all for your contributions.

A. THE SCOPE OF ACCOUNTING
Definitions of accounting
There are two definitions of accounting.
(i) Traditional View

From the tradition view, accounting has been defined as the process of collecting, arranging, processing, summarizing and presenting accounting data to the users of financial statements.
-Collecting involves calculating financial transactions.
-Arranging involves putting transaction in a good order form.
-Processing implies processing the transaction from the primary sources.
-Summarizing implies getting accounting information that is required.

(ii) Modern View:
From the modern view users of the information have defined accounting as the process of identifying, measuring and communicating economic information to permit informed judgments and decisions. This definition is good because it recognizes that accounting is a process, and that process is concerned with capturing business economic events, recording their financial activities, summarizing and reporting.

Note: The major focus of accounting today is to provide financial information for decision-making.

All organizations (large or small; manufacturing, retail or service, profit or non-profit making) have a need for accounting information. They use the information for decision-making.

The purpose of Accounting
The following are the summarized purposes of accounting:-
1. To determine profitability of the venture
2. Provide information to lenders
3. Taxation
4. Financial Planning
5. Decision Making
6. Report on the distribution of Resources
7. Public Interest

A business proprietor normally runs a business in order to: make profit. He or she needs information to know whether the business is doing well. The owner of a business might ask the following questions:

- How much profit or loss has the business made?
- How much money do owe?
- Will I have sufficient funds to meet my commitments?

The purpose of conventional business accounting is to provide the answers to such questions by presenting a summary of the transactions of the business in a standard form.

Financial accounting and management accounting

Accounting may be split into financial Accounting and management Accounting.

a) Financial Accounting
Financial accounting comprises two stages
- Book-keeping, which is the recording of day-to-day business transactions; and
- Preparation of accounts, of which is the preparation of statements from the bookkeeping records; these statements summaries the performance of the business-usually over the period of one year.

b) Management Accounting
The character Institute of Management Accounts (CIMA) defines management accounting as follows:

"The application of professional knowledge and skill in the preparation and presentation of accounting information in such a way as to assist management in the formulation of polices and in the planning and control of the operations of the undertaking.

Management accounting, therefore, seeks to provide information which will be used for decision-making purposes (e.g. pricing, investment), for planning and control.

Money as the Common Denominator
Accounting is concerned with money measurement-it is only concerned with information which can be given a monetary value. We put money values on its such as land, machinery and stock, and this is necessary for comparison purposes. For example, it is not very helpful to say: "last year we had four machines and 60 items of stock, and this year we have five machines and 45 items of stock." It is the money values which are useful to us.
There are, though, limitations to the use of money as the common denominator.

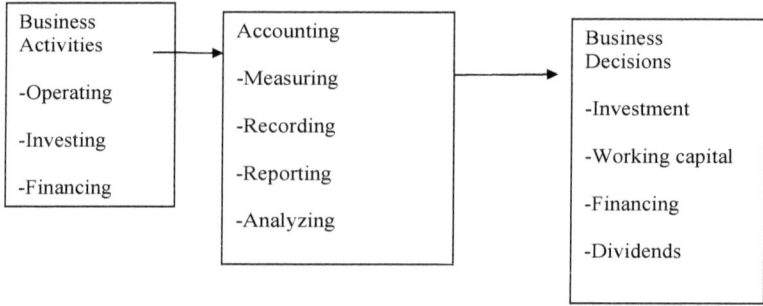

a. Human Ass

We have seen that accounting includes financial accounting and management accounting. Both of these make use of money measurement. However we may want further information about a business:

- Are industrial relations good or bad?
- Is staff morale high?
- Is the management item effective?
- What is the employment policy?
- Is there a responsible ecology policy?

These questions will not have answers by conventional business accounting in money terms but by "human asset accounting" and "social responsibility accounting". These issues have not yet been introduced and are outside the scope of our syllabus.

b. Devaluation

The value of money does not constant, and there is normally some degree of inflation in the economy. We will look at various steps that have been taken to attempt to adjust accounting statements to the changing value of money later.

The Business Entity

The business as accounting entity / (type of business) refers to the separate identities of the business and its proprietors.

- **The Sole Trader**

   There must always be a clear distinction between the owner of the business and the business itself. For example, if Mr. X owns a biscuit factory, we are concerned with recording the transactions of the factory. We are not concerned with what Mr. X spends on food and clothes. If Mrs. Y works at home, setting aside a room in her house, an apportionment may have to be made.

- **Partnership**

   Similarly, the partners in a business must keep the transactions of the business separate from their own personal affairs.

- **Companies**

   In law, a company has a "legal personality". This implies to the fact that a company may sue or be sued in its own right. The affairs of the shareholders must be distinguished from the business of the company. The proprietor of a limited company is there fore distinct from the company itself.

   We share return to the issue of business entities later in the unit.

7

B. USERS OF ACCOUNTING INFORMATION

We need to prepare accounts in order to "provide a statement that will meet the needs of the user, subject to the requirements of statute and case law and the accounting bodies, and aided by the experience of the reception of past report"

So if we prepare accounts to meet the needs of the user, **who is the user**?

Main Categories of Users

The main users of financial accounting information are Equity investors (shareholders, proprietors, buyers)

- Loan creditors (banks and other lenders)
- Employees
- Analysts/advisers
- Business contacts (creditors and debtors, competitors)
- The government (The Inland Revenue)
- The public
- Management (board of directors)

Users can learn a lot about the running of a company from the examination of its accounts, but each category of user will have its own special perspective. We need to look at some of these in more detail.

Users of accounting information are categorized into internal and external

External users of accounting information

-Investors, creditors, customers, taxing authorities, competitors and the Government.

Internal users of accounting information

-The Board of Directors, management, and employees.

Interests of principal users

- *Proprietor*
  The perspective of the business proprietor is explained above (but see bellow for the interests of shareholders)

- *Inland Revenue*

  The Inland Revenue will use the accounts to determine the liabilities of the businesses for taxation.

  These require knowing if the business is likely to be able to repay loans to settle, the interests charged. However, often the final accounts of a business do not tell the lender what he or she wishes to know. They may be several months old and so not show the up-to-date position. Under these circumstances, the lender will ask for cash low forecasts to show what is likely to happen in the business. This illustrates why accounting techniques have to be flexible and adaptable to meet users' needs.

- *Creditors and Debtors*

  These will often keep a close eye on the financial information provided by companies with which they have direct contact through buying and selling, to insure that their own businesses will not be affected by the financial failure of another. An indicator of trouble in this area is often information withheld at the proper time, though required by law. Usually, the longer the silence, the worse the problem becomes.

- *Competitors*

  Competitors will compare their own results with those of other companies. A company would not wish to disclose information, which would be harmful to its own business: equally, it would not wish to hide anything, which would put it above its competitors.

- *Board of Directors*

  The board of directors will up-to-date, in depth information so that it can draw up plans for the long term, the medium term and the short term, and compare results with its past decisions and forecasts. The board's information will be much more detailed than that which is published.

- **Shareholders**

  Shareholders have invested money to the company and as such, they are the owners of the business. Normally, a team of managers will run the company and the shareholders require the managers to account for their "stewardship" of the business, i.e. the use they have made of the shareholders' funds. In addition, they are interested to know a return on investment.

- **Employees**

  Employees of the company look for, among other things, security of employment and compensations.

- **Prospective Buyers**

  A prospective buyer of a business will want to see such information as will satisfy him or her that the price is a good as far as the ability of a firm to supply goods and / or services efficiently is concerned.

- **Lenders**
  They are interested to know the liquidity and solvency of a firm.

C. RULES OF ACCOUNTING (ACCOUNTING STANDARDS)

As different businesses use different methods of recording transactions, the result might be that financial accounts for different business would be very different in form and context. However, various standards for the preparation of accounts stated over a number of years. We shall be looking at the layout of financial accounts later on in the course. With regard to companies, various rules are incorporated into legislation (Companies Acts of the respective country). Companies whose shares are listed on the stock of exchange rules. There are also "statements of standard Accounting practice" (SSAPs) and Financial Reporting Statements (FRSs) which are issued by the main professional accounting bodies through the Accounting Standards Board (ASB).

Development of Accounting Standards

a. **Historical Development**
   In 1943, the institute of Chartered Accountings in England and Wales began to make recommendations about accounting practices, and over time issued a series of 29 Recommendations, in order to codify the best practice to be used in particular circumstances. Unfortunately, these recommendations did not reduce the diversity of accounting methods

- The Accounting Standards Committee
  In the late 1960s, there a lot of public criticism of financial reporting methods and the accounting profession responded to this by establishing the Accounting standards Committee (ASC) in 1970. The ASC comprised representatives of all the six major accounting bodies, i.e. the Chartered Accounts of England and Wales, of Scotland, and of Ireland, the certified Accounts, the cost and management accounts, and the Chartered institute of public financial and accountancy.

The Committee was set up to developing definitive standards for financial reporting.

A statement of intent produced in the 1970s identified the following objectives:

- ↟ To narrow the areas of difference in accounting practice
- ↟ Ensure disclosure of information on departures from definitive standards
- ↟ To provide a wide exposure for new accounting standards
- ↟ To maintain a continuing program for improving accounting standards.

Various accounting conventions (which we will look at later) lay down certain "ground rules" for accounting. However, they do still permit a variety of alternative practices to coexist. The lack of uniformity of practices made it difficult for users of financial reports to compare the results of different companies. There was therefore a need for standards of accounting practice, to try to increase the compatibility of company accounts.

- **Statements of Standard Accounting Practice (SSAP)**
  The procedure for their establishment was for the ASC to produce **an exposure draft** on a specific topic-e.g. accounting for stocks and depreciation-for comment by accounts and other users of accounting information. A formal statement was then drawn up, taking account of comments received, and issued as a **Statement of Standard Accounting Practice (SSAP)**. Once the accountancy profession had adopted a statement, any material departures by a company from the standard practice had to be disclosed in notes to the Annual Financial Accounts.

  These standards do not have the force of law to back them up, although all members of the accounting profession are required by their Code of Ethics to abide by them.

- **The Dearing Report**
  Although the ASC had much success during its period of operation and issued 25 SSAPs as well as a number of Exposure Drafts (EDs), Statements of Intent (SOI), and statements of Recommended Practice (SORP), there were many serious criticisms of its work, leading to its eventual demise.

  In July1987, the Consultative Committee of Accountancy Bodies (CCAB) set up a review of the standard-setting process under the leadership of Sir Ron Dearing. The **Dearing Report** subsequently made a number of very important recommendations. The government accepted all but one of them and in August 1990, a new standard setting structure was set up.

b. **The Accounting Standards Board**
   The following structure (Figure 1.1) as recommended by the Dearing Report, with the Financial Reporting Council (FRC) acting as the policy-making body for accounting standard setting.

   This gave rise to a slightly different regime for the establishment of standards and these are now included in the **Financial Reporting Standards (FRS)**

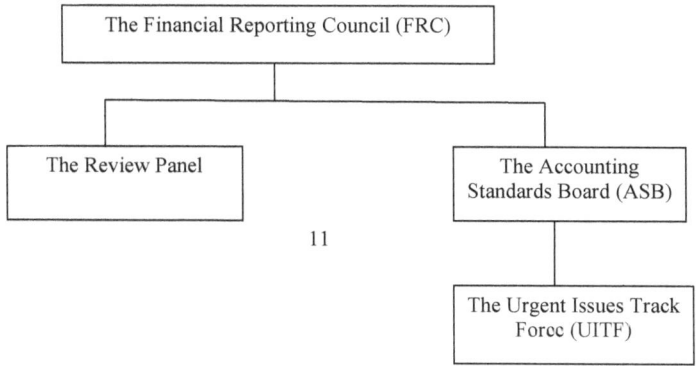

11

Figure 1.1 Standard Setting Structure

Financial Reporting Standards (FRS)
The ASB is more independent than the ASC was and can issue standards known as *Financial Reporting Standards* (FRS). The ASB accepted the SSAPs then in force and these remain effective until replaced by an FRS. The ASB develops its own exposure drafted along similar lines to the ASC; these are known as FREDs (Financial Reporting Exposure Drafts).

Statements of Recommended Practice (SORP)
Although the ASB believed that statement of recommended practice (SORPS) had a rule to pay, it did not adopt the SORPS already issued. Not to be diverted from its central task of developing accounting standards, the Board has left the development of SORPS to bodies recognized by the Board.

The SORPS issued by the ASC from 1986 different from SSAPs in that SSAPs had to be followed unless there were substantive reasons to prove otherwise, and non-compliance had to be clearly stated in the notes to the final accounts. A SORP simply sets out best practice on a particular topic for which a SSAP was not appropriate. However, the later SORPs are mandatory and cover a topic of limited application to a specific industry (e.g. local authorities, charities, housing associations). These SORPS as do not deviate from the basic principles of the various SSPs currently in issue.

Urgent issues Task Force (UITF)
This an offshoot of the ASB which tackles urgent matters not covered by existing standards or those which, if covered, were causing diversity of interpretation. In these circumstances, the UITF issues a "Pronouncement" in order to detect whether or not accounts give a true and fair view.

Financial Reporting Review Panel
This examines contentious departures from accounting standard by large companies. The panel has the power to apply to the court for an order requiring a company's directors to revise their accounts.

C. The International Accounting Standards Committee (IASC)

Apart from the UK Accounting standards, there are also standards issued by the international Accounting standards committee (IASC) which was established in 1973. Representatives from the United Kingdom sit on this committee with those of other countries. The need for the IASC arose because of International investment, the growth of multinational firms and the desire to have common standard worldwide. In the United Kingdom, our own standards take precedence over the IASC but most of the provision of IASs is already contained in existing SSAPs and FRSs. Where there is not –compliance with in IAS, this is the UK standard.

Statement of Standard Accounting Practice
Note that, with the issuing standards by the ASD (FRSs), there currently both a number of SSAPs and FRSs, but you should be aware of what they cover and we briefly review them here starting with SSAPs. Some of the more important standard will be dealt with in later study units under their own topic heading.

SSAP 1: Accounting for Associated Companies

Where one company has invested in another company and can significantly influence the affairs of that company, then rather simply show dividends received as a measure of income, the full share of the profits of that company should be shown in the investing company's accounts.

SSAP 2: Disclosure of Accounting practice
This standard requires if the accounts are prepared the basis of assumptions which differ materially from the generally accepted fundamental accounting concepts.

The position must be disclosed as a note to the accounts. (Accounting concepts are more fully covered later on in this study unit).

SSAP 3: Earnings Per Share
This SSAP defines how earning per share is calculated and is covered in more detail later in the course.

SSAP 4: Accounting for Government Grants
Grants should be recognized in the profit and loss account so as to match the expenditure to which they relate. Capital grants relating to capital expenditure should be credited to revenue over the expected useful economic life of the asset.

SSAP 5: Accounting for Value Added Tax
This aims to achieve uniformity of accounting treatment of VAT in financial statements.

SSAP 8: Treatment of Tax Under the Imputation System in Accounts of Companies
This establishes a standard treatment of taxation in company accounts with particular reference to advance and mainstream corporation tax.

SSAP 9: Stocks and Long-term Contracts
Stocks should be valued at the lower of cost or net realizable value. With long-term contracts the accounts should not recognize profit in advance but should account immediately for any anticipated losses (covered later in the course).

SSAP 12: Accounting for Depreciation
This SSAP applies to all fixed assets except investment properties, goodwill, development costs and investments. All assets with a finite life should be depreciated by allocating cost Less residual value to the revenue account, over their economic lives. The SSAP recognizes several different methods but does not insist on which method should be used; the method applied, however, should be consistent. (Covered later in the course)

SSAP 13: Accounting for Research and Development
Expenditure on pure (basic) or applied research can be regarded as ongoing to maintain a company's business. Expenditure on developing new and improved products is normally undertaken to secure future benefits, but should still also be written of in the year of expenditure unless it complies with stringent conditions, e.g. the project is commercially viable.

SSAP 15: Accounting for Deferred Tax
This covers the treatment of taxation attributable to timing differences between profits computed for tax purposes and profits as stated in financial statements. Timing differences originating in one period are likely to be reversed in a subsequent period.

SSAP 17: Accounting for Post Balance Sheet Events
Any event occurring up to balance sheet date will have affected the balance sheet, but normally it is impossible to alter the accounts after approval by the directors. However, between these two dates some types of events can be adjusted for, e.g. discovery of errors or frauds which shows that the financial statements were incorrect.

SSAP 18 Accounting for Contingencies
A contingency is a situation that exists at the balance sheet date, the outcome of which is uncertain. Contingent losses must be taken into account and the contingent gains left out. Material contingent losses can be disclosed in the notes to the balance sheet.

SSAP 19: Accounting for Investment Properties
This standard requires investment properties to be included in the balance sheet at open market value. Where investment properties represent a substantial proportion of the total assets the valuation should be out by a recognized professional person, and by an external value at least every five years.

SSAP 20: Foreign Currency Translation
This deals with the translation of foreign currency transactions from overseas branches or subsidiaries into sterling. The method used should be disclosed as a note to the final accounts.

SSAP 21: Accounting for Leases and Hire Purchase Contracts
This requires that a finance lease (where the lessee takes on the risks and rewards of ownership) should be accounted for by the lessee as if the asset had been purchased. In order words, substance over form.

SSAP 24: Accounting for Pension Costs
An employer recognize the cost of providing pensions on an equitable basis in relation to the period over which he derives benefit from services rendered by employees.

SSAP 25: Segmental Reporting
Information in accounts should be broken down by class of business and Geographically (covered later in the course).

Financial Reporting Standards

FRS 1: Cash Flow Statements
Cash flow statements replace the Source and Application of Funds Statement, to that the emphasis is now on what cash has in or out of the business during the Accounting period rather than on how the components of working capital have changed in the year. (See later in the course.)

FRS 2: Accounting for Subsidiary Undertakings
This deals with preparing accounts for parent and subsidiary companies.

FRS 3: Reporting Financial Performance
This covers the treatment of extraordinary and exceptional items in financial statements, and requires a statement of total recognized gains and losses to be prepared. (Covered later)

FRS 4: Accounting of Capital Instruments
This standard deals with the raising of finance.

FRS 5: Reporting the Substance of Transactions
This standard ensures that financial statements report the substance of transactions and not merely their legal form.

FRS 6: Accounting for Acquisitions and Mergers
This deals with the different accounting methods for acquisitions or mergers, including limiting the ability of a company to use merger accounting by setting out a number of conditions which must first be satisfied before merger accounting can be adopted.

FRS 7: Fair Values in Acquisition Accounting

All business combinations that do not quality as a merger in accordance with FRS 6 must therefore adopt acquisition accounting. This standard ensures that all the assets and liabilities of the acquire company at the date of acquisition are recorded at "fair Values" in the financial records of the acquiring company.

FRS 10: Accounting for Goodwill and Intangible Assets

Goodwill purchased should reflect the difference between the price paid for a business and the fair value of the net assets acquired. Goodwill should not include any value for intangible items; these should be included under the heading of intangible assets in the balance sheet. Purchased goodwill should not remain as a permanent item in the balance sheet. It must be mortised against profit and loss in ordinary activities over its useful economic life. (This is covered in more detail later in the course.

D. ACCOUNTING PERIODS.

An owner of a business will require financial information at regular intervals. As we have noted, he or she will want to be able to check periodically how well or badly the business is doing. Financial accounts are normally prepared on an annual basis, e.g. twelve months to the 31 march. Preparing accounts on annual basis facilitates comparisons between one year and previous years and assists forecasting the next year. For example, there many be seasonal factors affecting the business, which will even out over the year. An ice-cream vendor will expect to make more sales in the summer months than in the winter months. He would not be able to tell if business is improving by looking at accounts for six months ended 31 march 20XX and comparing them with accounts for the six months ended 30 September 20XX. True comparison of profit/loss can be gained only when he examines this account for the years (say) 31 march 20X1 and 31 March 20X2.

Accounts normally have to be prepared annually for tax purposes as tax is assessed on profits of a 12-month accounting period. In the case of limited companies, accounts are prepared annually to the "accounting reference date". It is necessary to calculate annually the amount of profit available for distribution to shareholders by way of divided.

E.THE FUNDAMENTAL CONCEPTS OF ACCOUNTING

Statement of standard Accounting practice No. 2 is called *Disclosure of Accounting polices*. It identifies four fundamental accounting concepts which should be followed in preparing accounts. These four concepts are also included in company law so companies must follow them in preparing published accounts. These concepts are known as the accruals, prudence, going concern and consistency concepts.

Accruals

Accruals is taking into account or **matching** income and expenditure occurring within an accounting period, whether actual cash is received or paid during the time or not. The reasoning behind the concept is that profit for the period should represent fairly the earrings of the time covered and, in view of the dynamic nature of any business; it is unlikely that all invoices will have been paid. However, they should be accounted for to give a true picture.

A distinction is made between the receipt of cash and the right to receive cash, and between the payment of cash and the legal obligation to pay cash. The accruals concept requires the accountant to include as expenses or income those sums which are due and payable.

You need to remember what the following terms mean.

> **Receipt**: the receipt of cash or cheques by the business, normally in return for good or serves rendered. The receipt may relate to another financial period, e.g. it may be for goods sold at the end of the previous period.
> **Payment**: the payment of cash or cheques by the business in return for goods or services received. A gain, a payment may be in respect of goods purchased in the previous financial year or a service to be rendered in the future, e.g. rates payable in advance.

Additionally, the term "capital receipt" is used to describe amounts received from the sale of fixed assets or investments, and similarly: capital payment" might relate to an amount paid for the purchase of a fixed (i.e. long-term) asset.

> **Revenue income**: the income which a business earns when it sells its goods. Revenue is recognized when the goods pass to the customer, NOT when the customer pays.
> **Expenses**: these include all resources used up or incurred by a business during a financial year irrespective of when they are paid for. They include salaries, wages, rates, rent, telephone, stationary, etc.

To help you understand the significance of these terms, here are a few examples (financial year ending 31 December):

> Telephone bill £200 paid January year 2 relating to previous quarter = Payment years2; Expense year 1.
> Debtors pay £ 500 in January Year 2 for goods supplied (sales) in Year 1= Receipt Year 2 Revenue Income Year 1.
> Rent paid £ 1,000 July Year 1 for period 1 July Year 1 to Year 2= Payment £1,000 Year 1; Expense Year 1 £500, Expense Year 2£500.

In a later study unit we will see how these matters are dealt with in the final accounts.

Accounting Prudence

Prudence is proper caution in measuring profit and income.

Whereby sales are in cash, profit and income have to be accounted for in full. Whereby sales are in credit basis, however, the question of the certainty of profits or incomes arises. If there is not a good chance of receiving money in full, no sales are made on credit anyway; but if, in the interval between the sale and the receipt of cash, it becomes doubtful that the cash will be received, prudence dictates that a full provision for the sum outstanding should be made. A provision being an amount which is set aside via the profit and loss account.

The two main aspects of this concept are that;

Income has not to be anticipated and all possible losses should be provided for.
The method of valuation of an asset, which gives the lesser value, has to be chosen.

Prudence is often exercised subjectively on grounds of experience and is likely, in general, to lead to an understatement of profit. The subjectivity involved can lead to variation between accountants in the amount of provision for bad debts, etc. and is bound to create differences between results obtained by the same general method of management. Users are differences between results of various businesses, which although apparently comparable, in fact conceal individual distortions.

In long-term credit arrangements, e.g. hire-purchase agreements, difficulties arise in the actual realization of income and profit. The date of the sale, whether on a cash or credit basis, is usually regarded as the date of realization; but if you have money coming in over two or three years, measurement of the actual sum realized is subject to controversy.

Going Concern

This concept assumes that the business is going on steadily trading from year to year without reducing its operations.

You can often see if an organization is in financial trouble, e.g. if it lacks working capital, and in these circumstances it would not be correct to follow this concept. It would probably be better to draw up a statement of affairs, valuing assets on a break-up basis rather than reflecting the business as a going concern (i.e. on the basis of a sudden sale of all the assets, where the sale prices of the assets would be less than on ordinary sale).

Including of other potential liabilities might be necessary to reflect the situation properly, e.g. payments on redundancy, pensions accrued, liabilities arising because of non-completion of contracts. Thus, the going concern concept directly influences values, on whatever basis they are measured.

Management must give their opinion on the going concern status of an entity for at least 12 months from the date of preparing the financial statements

Accounting Consistency

This is one of the most useful concepts from the point of view of users who need to follow accounting statements from year to year. Put simply, it involves using **unvarying accounting treatments** from one accounting period to the next e.g. in stock valuation, etc

Better eradicate if not avoid big *variances*, since big variances signifies accounting problems especially fraud practices in that accounting period.(This is to any kind of a business venture)

If only if: there are not enough explanations reported by the accounting members.

You can only identify a trend with certainty if accounts are consistent over long periods; otherwise, the graph of a supposed trend may only reflect a lack of precision or a change of accounting policies. However, there will usually be changes or inconsistencies in accounting policies over the years and in public accounts it is essential to stress these changes so that users can make proper allowance for differences.

Uniformity in financial reporting. An accounting practice adopted in one accounting period should be used in consequent accounting periods. A change in accounting policy must be justified – enables the financial statements to present the true and fair view. Expenses, assets, liabilities and revenues should not be reclassified in consequent accounting periods.

Substance Over Form

In case of variation between the legal aspect of a transaction and the financial reality of such transaction, the financial reality prevails.

Example - Hire purchase

Legal position: we own the assets when we pay the last instalment.

Financial Reality: we are using the asset to generate income and so it should be treated as part of the assets we own.

Money Measurement

Financial statements should reflect only those transactions that can be quantified in monetary terms.

Accruals (Matching)

Involves matching of costs with the revenue they generate. Has a direct effect on the profits and the cash flow position. Revenues are recognized when there is reasonable evidence that the firm has a right to it e.g. Goods have been provided to the buyer. Expenses are recognized when incurred.

Departures from SSAP 2

Because there are situations where even these four fundamental concepts do not hold true, SSAP 2 permits departures from these concepts, provided that the reasons are disclosed for any non-compliance with the standard.

The main difficulty in applying fundamental accounting concepts arises from the fact that many business transactions have financial effects spreading over a number of years. Decisions have to be made on the extent to which expenditure incurred in one year can reasonably be expected to produce benefits in the form of revenue in other years and should therefore be carried, in whole or in part. In other words, should it be dealt with in the closing balance sheet, as distinct from being dealt with as an expense of the current year in the profit and loss account because the benefits has been exhausted in that year?

In some cases revenue is received for goods or services the production or supply of which will involve some later expenditure. In this case a decision must be made regarding how much of the revenue should be carried forward, to be dealt with in subsequent profit and loss accounts when the relevant costs are incurred.

All such decisions required consideration of future events of uncertain financial effect, and to this extent an element of commercial judgment is unavoidable. Examples of matters which give rise to particular difficulty are:-

> The future benefits to be derived from stocks and all types of work-in-progress at the end of the year.
> The future benefits to be derived from fixed assets, and the period of years over which these will be fruitful.
> The extent to which expenditure on research and development can be expected to produce future benefits.

Accounting Bases and Policies

SSAP 2 also identified accounting bases, or methods of dealing with certain items.

In the course of practice, a variety of accounting bases have develop which are designed to provide consistent, fair and as nearly as possible objective solutions to problems; for example, bases for calculating depreciation and the amounts at which stocks can be stated.

Accounting bases provide an orderly and consistent framework for periodic reporting of a concern's results and financial position, but they do not, and are not intended to, substitute for commercial judgment in the preparation of financial reports. Where a choice in accounting base is a available, judgment must be exercised in choosing those that are best suited to present fairly the concern's results and financial position. The bases thus adopted then become the concern's accounting policies.

OTHER ACCOUNTING CONCEPTS.

Money Measurement

Whether in historic or current terms, money is used as the unit of account to express information on a business and, from analysis of the figures; assumptions can be made by the users.

As we have seen, through, this concept of a common unit goes only some way towards meeting user need, through, and further explanation is often needed on non-monetary requirements, e.g. the experience of the management team, lab our turnover, social policy.

Duality

Each item in a business has two accountancy aspects, reflected in the accounting treatment, for example:

Double entry bookkeeping requires each transaction to be entered twice as a debit and as a credit. The debit being an increase in the assets of the company or as an expense, the credit entry being a reduction in the cash balance, to pay for the item, or an increase in the item, or an increase in the level of credit taken.

Assets of a business are shown in one section of a balance sheet and the liabilities in another.

There is little to criticize in this duality but we are looking behind the framework at the efficiency of the system and judging it by its success in meeting user needs. Duality falls short in the same sphere as money measurement, because there are areas in which it is not relevant.

Matching

Often considered the accruals concept, matching calls for the revenue earned in a period to be linked with related costs. This gives rise to accruals and prepayment which account for the difference between cash flow and profit and loss information. This distinction will be clarified when you look at examples later.

Cost

As money is used to record items in the business accounts, each item has a cost.

Accountants determine the value of an asset by reference to its purchase price, not to the value of the returns which are expected to be realized. Many problems are raised by this convention, particularly in respect of the effect of inflation upon asset values.

This can also be considered as the historic cost concept.

Materiality

Accounting for every single item individually in the accounts of a muti-million pound concern would not be cost-effective.

A user would gain no benefit from learning that a stock figure of £ 200,000 included £ 140 work-in-progress as distinct from raw materials. Neither would it make much difference that property cost £ 429,872 rather than the £ 430,000. Indeed, rounded figures give clarity to published statements. So, when they are preparing financial statements, accountants do not concern themselves with minor items. They attempt rather to prepare clear and sensible accounts.

The concept of materiality therefore leaves itself open to the charge that accounts so prepared are not strictly accurate, but generally the advantages outweigh this shortcoming.

Stability of Money Value

There is a certain amount of conflict here between the economist and the accountant. It is common knowledge that the £of yesterday will not have the same value as the £ of tomorrow, but the accountant knows that he must be as practical as possible and whilst he accept the different values, he knows that to incorporate them into the structure of his accounts would cause problems.

Any form of inflationary accounting has its inaccuracies. All that can really be said about accounting for inflation is that it provides a better measure of the true economic situation than historic accounts. The latter are still used for tax computations and are, in most instances, the sort required by law. There is no compulsory requirement for accounting for changing price levels.

Objectivity

Financial statements should be produced **free from bias** (not a rosy picture to a potential lender and a poor result for the taxman, for instance). Reports should be capable of verification - a difficult problem with forecasts.

Realization

Any change in the value of an asset may not be recognized until the moment the firm realizes or disposes of that asset. For example, even if a sale is on credit, we recognize **the revenue** as soon as the goods are passed to the customer.

However, unrealized gains, such as increases in the value of stock prior to resale, are now widely recognized by non-accountants, (e.g. bankers) and this can lead to problems with this concept.

Business Entity Concept

22

The affairs of the business are distinguished from the personal affairs of the owner(s). Thus a separate capital account is maintained in the business books, which records the business's indebtedness to the owner(s).

It is important to draw a clear a distinction between the owner of a business and the business and the business itself. As far as accountancy is concerned, the record of the business are kept with a view to controlling and recording the affairs of the business and not for any benefit to the owner, although the completed account will be presented to the owners for their information.

However it is sometimes hard to divorce the two interests, especially when you are dealing with the sole trader, whose affairs are intertwined with the business he owns and is operating. So if, for example, he owns a sweetshop and takes and eats a bar of chocolate, he is anticipating his profit - as he is if he takes a few pence from the till to pay for some private purchase; and such activities should be recorded. His more personal affairs, however, such as the cost of food, clothing and heat and light for his private residence, must be kept separately from the business records.

When we look at **the partnership** the distinction becomes a little clearer; and when we look at **limited companies**, where the owners or shareholders may takes no part in running the company and the law gives the company a distinct legal personality of its own, then we have a clear-cut division and it is easy to distinguish owner and business.

D. IMPORTANT ACCOUNTING TERMS

The Accounting Equation or Basic Formula

In any business, there are two categories: the business and its owner/s. Capital is provided by the owners in the form of goods, and this capital is normally used by the business to acquire assets and finance its operations.   When accounts are kept / written, the balance sheet will show the assets of the business, net of any liabilities not yet settled, balanced against the owners' capital. We can therefore say that:

Capital= Total Assets (i.e. Total Assets -Total Liabilities)

The **capital** is what belongs to the owner/s, and the **net assets** are the assets used in the business. Should the business cease those net assets will have to be used in order to raise the cash to repay the owners' capital.

As a business progresses both the net assets and the owner's capital increase. Let us assume that an owner invests £10,000in a business. The opening balance in the balance sheet will therefore show:

Capital £10,000=Net assets (cash at bank) £10,000

If a business is successful over the years, the figures will increase, so that after a period we may see, for example:

Capital £20,000=Net assets £20,000

This equation is called:- the **basic formula** and you will notice that both sides have equal values. This is because all modern accounting record keeping is based on the **principle of double entry**. This means that every transaction in the account **must** have two entries, a debit entry in one account and a credit in another.

Assets and Liabilities

Net assets represent the assets of the business after deducting outstanding liabilities due to third parties. To calculate the net assets we take the **total assets** and deduct the **liabilities**.

- **Assets** are the property of the business and include land and buildings, cash, debtors and money in the bank.
  Resource controlled by the entity as a result of past events and from which future economic benefits are expected to flow in the entity.
  Conditions:
  1. Owned by the entity – Entity controls it
  2. Future economic benefit
     Transaction to acquire has taken
- **Liabilities** are what the business owes to outside firm for goods or service supplied, loans made or expenses.
- Liabilities are debts.
- Long-Term Liabilities – Debts expected to be repaid over one financial year. Bank loans, debentures, mortgages.
- Short-Term Liabilities – Debts that have to be repaid within the financial year. Trade creditors, bank overdrafts, expense accruals.

You can relate this to your own situation. You probably own various assets – perhaps a flat, a car, and some household effects. At the same time you may well owe money to a credit card company, the newsagent or a finance company. If you are an employee then your employer will owe you money by way of salary or wages. When you are in business then the business will owe you money by way of your capital and profits.

The treatment and classification of assets and liabilities in the accounts is of fundamental importance:

- **Assets** involve expenditure and are always shown as debit entries in the accounts. There are two main classes of assets:
  (i) **Fixed assets,** which comprise land and buildings, plant and machinery, motor vehicles, fixture and fittings – in fact any assets, which are to be used in the business for a reasonable period generally, taken to be greater than one year.
  (ii) **Current assets,** which consist of stock for resale, debtors, cash/bank. Current assets are short – term assets, not intended to be retained in the business for long.

(Note that expenses also involve expenditure and are always shown as debit entries.)

- **Liabilities** consist of money owing for:
  (i) Good purchased on credit
  (ii) Expenses owing for items like telephone bills, unpaid garage bills, etc.
  (iii)Loans from, say, the bank societies, hire purchase, etc.

Capital v. Revenue Expenditure

When assets such as buildings, plant and machinery, motor vehicle, tools, etc. are bought, they are purchased not for resale but for use in running the business. This type of asset is known as a **fixed asset.** Fixed assets help to create profit, and expenditure on them is known as **capital expenditure**.

As well as the cost of the asset there are addition costs such as carriage on machinery or the legal costs of acquiring land and buildings. If a prefabricated building is erected, there would be additional costs such as the materials used (cement and bricks for the foundations), and the lab our costs incurred to erect the building. All these costs are included in the cost of the builing and are referred to as **capital expenditure**. This class of expenditure is kept separate from revenue expenditure, which relates to the day-to-day running of the business. Examples of **revenue expenditure** include expenses such as petrol for the vans, telephone charges for the sales department, etc.

You should have no difficulty in distinguishing between capital and revenue expenditure. Remember that capital is spent to buy fixed asset which are used to create profits, while revenue is spend in the creation of profit. We will remind you of the difference between these two types of expenditure in later study units.

Effects of Not Complying With the Rule

If we include fixed assets in revenue expenditure, we will reduce the profit and at the same time fail to disclose the fixed assets. This in turn means that any depreciation (see later in course) will not be taken. If we add revenue items in the fixed assets, we have the opposite effect, i.e. more profit and depreciation incorrectly charged.

The **Companies Act 1989** includes the following directive in relation to published company accounts:

> 'The balance sheet shall give a true fair view of the state of affairs as at the end of the financial year. The profit and loss account shall give a true and fair view of the profit of loss of the company for the financial year'

If we mix capital and revenue expenditure, not only will the accounts be incorrect but they will also contravene the law.

E. DIFFERENT TYPES OF BUSINESS ENTITY

We can now return to the issue of business entities and distinguish them in more sophisticated ways.

The Sole Trader

A sole trader is a business person trading on his or her own account. A sole trader bears total responsibility for business debits and , if in difficulty, may even need to sell personal assets to discharge liabilities.

A sole trader is a business which is owned by one person, although we should remember that the business may employ several others. Capital is introduced by the owner and the profits will be used in two main ways:

- As drawing (the proprietor's wages).
- As retention of profits which will be used to finance the business in future.

Partnerships

A partnership is group of people working together with a view to generating a profit. The basic structure of a partnership is governed by the **Partnership Act 1890**. There will often be a deed of partnership which lays down in writing the rights and responsibilities of the individual partners, but there is no legal requirement for any partnership agreement to be put into writing.

There are types of partnership:

a) Ordinary or General Partnership

This consist of a group of ordinary partners, each of whom contributes an agreed amount of capital, with each being entitled to participate in the business activity and to share profits within an agreed profit-sharing ratio. Each partner is jointly liable for debits of the partnership unless there is some written agreement to the contrary. This is the most common form of partnership.

b) Limited Partnership

This must consist of at least one ordinary partner to take part in the business, and to be fully liable for debits as if it were an ordinary partnership. Some partners are limited partners who May take no part in the business activity and whose liability is limited to the capital which they have agreed to put in. Such firms have to be registered and are not common.

Limited Companies

There are four main characteristics, which distinguish limited company:

- The legal nature of the business
- Statutory rules governing the form and content of published accounts
- Separation of ownership from the management of business
- Limited liability of the shareholders

A company is completely separate in law from its shareholders and as such it may be sued in the courts. On its formation the shareholders subscribe for shares in the company in return for money (or money's worth). The shareholders then collectively own the company and are entitled to share in the profits generated by it.

Several types of limited companies exist:

(a) Private Companies
These must comprise one or more members (shareholders) and may not offer shares to the public at large. A private company's name must end with "Limited" or "Ltd".

(b) Public companies

A public company is a company limited by shares which must have at least two members and an authorized capital of at least £50,000, at least one quarter of which must be paid up. There is no maximum number of members prescribed and the company can offer its shares to the public. A public company's name must end with the words "public limited company" or "plc"

(c) Quoted companies

Quoted (listed) companies are those whose shares are exchanged (bought and sold) on a recognized stock exchange Market. Large organizations may have a full listing on the London Stock Exchange, whilst smaller firms have to be listed on the Alternative Investment Market. The latter was established to provide a market for younger companies, which could not afford the costs of a full listing on the Stock Exchange Market listing.

(d) Unquoted companies
These are companies:- which do not have a full listing on recognized exchange. An unquoted company may be a private or a public company and some shares may be traded through the Alternative Investment Market.

Accounting Differences between Companies and Unincorporated Businesses

The following table summarizes the main accounting differences between the alternative types of business:

Item	Sole Traders and Partnerships	companies
Capital introduced	To the capital account	As issued share capital
Profits withdrawn by the owners	As drawings	As dividends
Profits left in the business	In a capital account	As a revenue reserve
Loans made from outside investors	As loan accounts	As loan accounts
		As dividend

Principle of Limited Liability

The principle of limited liability means that a member agrees to take shares in a company up to a certain amount, and once he has paid the full price for those shares he is not responsible for any debits that the company may the incur, if it becomes insolvent within a few months of his becoming a member.

This provides a safeguard against the private personal estate of a member being attached to make good the company's debits. (Remember sole traders and partners in such circumstances can lose the whole of their business and private wealth.)

Promoters and Legal Documents

Promoters are the people who comply with the necessary formalities of company registration. They find directors and shareholders, acquire business assets and negotiate contracts. They draw up the memorandum and article of the new company and register them with the Registrar of Companies.

The **memorandum of association** is said to the "charter" of the company it must state the company's objects as well as other detail such as its name and address and details of authorized capital.

The **articles of association** are the internal regulations or by-laws of the company, dealing with such matters as the issue and forfeiture of shares, procedure at meetings, shareholders' voting powers, and appointment, qualification, remuneration and removal directors.

When the promoters have arranged all the formalities and satisfied themselves that the statutory regulations have been complied with, they apply for a **certificate of incorporation** which brings the company into existence as a legal being, known as a registered company.

A. CAPITAL OF A COMPANY.

Virtually every business must have capital subscribed by its proprietors to enable it to operate. In the case of a partnership, the contribute capital up to agreed amounts which are credited to their account and shown as separate liabilities in the balance sheet.

A limited company obtain its capital, to the it is authorized to issue, from its members. A public company, on coming into existence, issues **a prospectus** inviting the public to subscribe for shares. The prospectus advertises the objects and prospect of the company in the most tempting manner possible. It is then up to the public to decided whether they wish to apply for shares.

A private company is not allowed to issue a prospectus and obtain its capital by means of **personal introductions** made by the promoters.

Once the capital has been obtained, It is lumped together in one sum and credited to **share capital account.** This account does not show how shares were subscribed by A or B; such information is given in the register of members which is a statutory book that all companies must keep but which forms no part of the double-entry book-keeping.

Features of share capital

- Once it has been introduced into the company, it generally cannot be repaid to the shareholders (although the shares may change hands). An exception to this is redeemable shares.

- Each share has stated **nominal** (sometimes called **par**) value. This can be regarded as the lowest price at which the share can be issued.
- Share capital of the company may be divided into various classes, and the articles of association defined the respective rights of the various shares as regards, for example, entitlement to dividends or voting at company meetings.

Type of share
(a) Ordinary Shares

The holder of ordinary shares in a limited company possesses no special right other than the ordinary right of every shareholder to participate in any available profits. If no divided is declared for a particular year, the holder of ordinary shares receives no return on his shares for that year. On the other hand, in a high profit he may receive a much higher rate of dividend than other classes of shareholders. Ordinary shares are often called equity share capital or just equities.

Deferred ordinary shareholders are entitled to divide after preferred ordinary shares.

(b) Preference Shares

Holders of preface shares are entitled to a prior claim, usually at a fixed rate, on any profit available for dividend. Thus when profits are small, preference shareholders must first receive their dividend at the fixed rate per cent, and any surplus may then be available for a dividend on the ordinary shares – the rate per cent depending, of course, on the amount of profits available. So as long as the business is making a reasonable profit, a preference shareholder is sure of a fixed return each year on his investment. The holder of ordinary shares may receive a very low dividend in one year and a much higher one in another.

Preference shares can be dividend into two classes:

- ### *Cumulative Preference Shares*

When a company is unable to pay dividends on this type of preference share in any one year, or even in successive years, all arrears are allowed to accumulate and are payable out of future profits as they become available.

- ### *Non-cumulative Preference Share*

If the company is unable to pay the fixed dividend in any one year, dividends on non-cumulative preference shares are not payable out of profits in future years.

(c) Redeemable Shares

The company`s articles association may authorize the issue of redeemable shares. These are issued with the intention of being redeemed at some future date. On redemption the company repays the holders of such shares(provided they are fully paid –up) out of a special reserve fund of assets or from the proceeds of a new issue of shares which is made expressly for the purpose of redeeming the shares previously issued. Redeemable shares may be preference or ordinary shares.

(d) Participating reference Shares

These are preference shares which are entitled to the usual dividend at the specified rate and, in addition, to participate in the remaining profits. As a general rule, the participating preference shareholders take their fixed dividend and then the preferred ordinary shareholders take their fixed dividend, and any balance remaining is shared by the participating preference and ordinary shareholders in specified proportions

Deferred, Founder or Management Share

As loan account   As loan accoun

These normally rank last of all for dividend. Such shares are usually held by the original owner of a business which has been take over by a company, and they often form part or even the whole of the purchase price. Dividends paid to holders of deferred shares may fluctuate considerably, but in prosperous time they may be a high rate.

You should note that this type of share has nothing to do with employee share schemes, where employees are given or allowed to buy ordinary shares in the company for which they work, at favorable rates – i.e. at less than the market quotation on the Stock Exchange.

Types of capital

(d) **Authorized, Registered or Nominal**.

These terms are synonymously used for capital that is specified as being the maximum amount of capital which the company has power to issue. Authorized capital must be stated in detail as a note to the balance sheet.

(e) Issued (Allocated) or Subscribed Capital

It is quate a regular practice for companies to issue only part of their authorized capital. The term "issued capital" or "subscribed capital" is used to refer to the amount of capital which has actually been subscribed for. Capital falling under this heading will comprise all shares issued to the public for cash and those issued as fully – paid – up to the Vendors of any business taken over by the company.

(f) Called-up Capital

The payment of the amount due on cash share is not always made in full on issue, but may be made in stages – for example, specified amount on application and a further amount when the shares are actually allotted, with the balance in one or more instilments known as **calls**. Thus, payment for a £1 share may be made as follows:

- 25p on application
- 25pon allotment
- 25p on first call
- 15p on second call
- 10pon third and
- Final call.

If a company does not require all cash at once on shares issued, it may call up what it needs. The portion of the subscribed capital which has actually been requested by the company is known as they called –up capital.

Note that a shareholder's only liability in the event of the company's liquidation is pay up any portion of his shred which the company has not fully called up. If a shareholder has paid for his shares, he has **no further liability**.

(g) Paid-up Capital

When a company makes a call, some shareholders may default and not pay the amount requested. Thus the amount actually paid up will not always be the same as the called-up capital. For example, suppose a company has called up 75p per share on its authorized capital of 20,000 £1shares. The called-up capital is £15,000, but if some shareholders have defaulted, the actual amount paid up may be only £14,500. In this case, the paid-up capital is £14,500, and the called-up capital £ 15,000. Paid up capital is therefore the amount paid on the called-up capital.

(e). Uncalled Capital or Called-up Share Capital Not paid.

If, as in our example, a company has called up 75 per share on its authorized capital of £20,000 £1 shares, there uncalled capital is the amount not yet required on shares already issued and partly paid for by the public and vendors. In this example the uncalled capital is £5,000.

Share Issues.

When a company issues shares, it can call for the whole value of the share or shares bought to be paid in one lump sum, or it can request the payment to be made in installments. Generally, a certain amount is paid upon application, a certain amount on each of a number of calls (the installments). For our purposes we only need to look at shares which are payable in full upon application.

32

(a). Shares at Par

This means that the company is asking the investor to pay the normal value, e.g. if a company issues 100,000 ordinary shares at £1, which is the par value, then the cash received will be £100,000. We can follow the entries in the accounts:

	Dr	Cr	
	£	£	
Cash	**100,000**		
Share capital		100,000	

The balance sheet will show:	
	£
Current assets	
Cash	£100,000
Share capital	
Authorized, issued and fully paid 100,000 £1 shares	£100,000

The basic rules of double entry apply and as you can see the basic formula is the same:

Capital (£100,000) = Net assets (Cash: £100,000)

(b). Shares at a Premium

A successful company, which is paying good dividends or which has some other favorable feature, may issue shares at a price which is higher than the normal value. For example, as in the last example, if the £1 share is issued it may be that the applicant will be asked to pay £1.50. The additional amount is known as a premium.

The entries in the accounts will now be:

	Dr	Cr	
	£	£	
Cash	150,000		
Share capital		100,000	
Share premium account		50,000	

The balance sheet will show:

	£
Current assets	
Cash	£150,000
Share capital	
Authorized, issued and fully paid 100,000 £1 shares	£100,000
Share premium account	150,000

Notes:

- The share premium is treated separately from the nominal value and must be recorded in a separate account which must be shown in the balance sheet. The Companies Act requires that the account is to be called the share premium account, and sets strict rules as to the uses to which this money can be put.
- The basic formula will now be:

Capital (£150,000) = Net Assets (Cash: £150,000)

And this means that the additional sum paid belongs to the shareholders and as such must always be shown together with the share capital.

Bonus Issues.

When a company has **substantial undistributed profits**, the capital employed in the business considerably greater than the issued capital. To bring the two more into line it is common practice to make a bonus issue of shares. Cash is not involved and it adds nothing to the net assets of the company-it simply **divides the real capital into a larger number of shares.** This is illustrated by the following example.

A company's balance sheet is as follows:

	£000
Net assets	1,000
Ordinary shares	500
Undistributed	500
	1,000

We can see that the real value of each share is £2, i.e.net assets £1,000÷500, but note that this is **not** the market value – only what each share is worth in terms of net assets owned compared with the nominal value of £1. Now suppose the company issued bonus shares on the basis of one new share for each existing share held. The balance sheet will now be as follows:

	£000
Net assets	1,000
Ordinary shares	1,000

Each shareholder has **twice as many shares** as before but is no better off since he owns exactly the same assets as before. All that has happened is that the share capital represents all the net assets of the company. This does, dilute the equity of the ordinary shareholders, but more substantial share account can often enable a company to obtain further finance from other sources. It can also be used as a defense against takeover because the bidder cannot there by obtain control and distribute the reserves.

Rights Issues.

A useful method of **raising fresh capital** is first to **offer new shares to existing shareholders, at something less than the current market price of the share** (provided that this is higher than the nominal value). This is a right issue, and it is normally based on number of shares held, as with a bonus issue, e.g. one for ten. In this case, however, there is no obligation on the part of the existing shareholder to take advantage of the rights offer, but if he does the shares have issued to be paid for. **The Companies** Act requires that, before any equity shares are issued for cash they must first be offered to current shareholders.

Example

A company with an issued share capital of £500,000 in £1 ordinary shares decides to raise an additional £100,000 by means of a one- for-ten right issue, at a price of £2 per share. The issue is fully subscribed and all moneys are received. The book-keeping entries are:

Dr:	Cash	£100,000	
Cr:	Share capital a/c		£50,000
Cr:	Share premium a/c		£50,000

Note the credit to shares premium account. You should also note that neither bonus nor rights issues can be allotted if they would cause the authorized capital to be exceeded.

Redeemable Shares

Redeemable shares may not be issued at a time when there are no issued shares of the company which are not redeemable. This means that there must be at all times some shares which are not redeemable.

Only **fully-paid shares** may be redeemed and, if a premium is paid on redemption, then normally the premium must be paid be out of distributable profits, unless the premium effectively represents a repayment of capital because it was share premium paid when the shares were issued. In that case the share premium may be paid from the share premium account.

When shares are redeemed, the redemption payments can make either:

(a) From the proceeds of a new issue of shares, or

(b) From profits.

If (b) is chosen then an amount equal to the value of the shares redeemed has to be transferred from the distributable profits to an account known as the **capital redemption reserve.**

The Act makes it clear that when shares are redeemed it must not be taken that there is a reduction of the company's **authorized** share capital.

By issuing redeemable shares the company is creating temporary membership which comes to an end either after a fixed period or at the shareholder's or company 's option. When the temporary membership comes to an end the shares that are redeemed must be cancelled out. To avoid the share capital contributed being depleted, replenishment must be made as mentioned earlier, i.e. by an issue of fresh shares or by a transfer from the profit and loss account.

(**Note**: In the illustration which follows we have adopted a "standard" balance sheet which we will discuss later. For the present, you need not be concerned with regard to how the balance sheet is constructed.)

Example.

On 31 July the balance sheet of Health field Industries plc was as follows:

	£	£
Fixed assets		135,000
Current assets	47,000	
Current liabilities	(12,000)	35,000
		170,000
Capital and Reserves		
40,000 £1 ordinary shares		40,000
30,000 redeemable £1 shares fully paid		30,000
Profit and loss account		100,000
		170,000

Notes

- The bank balance which is included in the current assets stands at £20,000.

37

- It is the intention of the directors to redeem £15,000 of the redeemable shares, **the redemption being made by cash held at the bank.**

After the redemption the balance sheet would look like this:

	£	£
Fixed assets		135,000
Current assets	32,000	
Current liabilities	(12,000)	20,000
		155,000
Capital and Reserves		
40,000 £1 ordinary shares		40,000
15,000 £1 redeemable shares		15,000
Capital redemption fund *		15,000
Profit and loss account		85,000
		155,000

- Under the **Companies Act,** When redeemable shares are redeemed and the funds to redeem are **not** provided by a new issue of shares i.e. the cash is available, then should be a transfer which is illegal other than by statutory procedures.

Notes:

- You will see that the basic formula is not changed. We still have:

    Capital £170,000 = net assets £170,000

And after an equal amount has been taken from both sides (the reduction in cash and a reduction in the redeemable shares) we have:

Capital £155,000 = Net assets £155,000

- There are very strict rules regarding the capital redemption reserve and the only transfer without court approval is by way of creating **bonus shares**.

38

- Don't worry about the profit and loss account because we will discuss this account fully in a later study unit.
- You may wonder why there are so many strict rules. This because **Companies Act** are there to protect **the shareholders.**

Purchase of Own Shares

The **Companies Act** authorizes a company to purchase its own shares provided that it is so authorized by its **articles**. There are three main rules:

(a) It may purchase, but this does not mean subscribe for, shares.
(b) It cannot purchase all its shares leaving only redeemable shares.
(c) Shares may not purchase unless they are **fully paid.**

Note: Redeeming or purchasing shares may appear to be the same thing, particularly as the same accounting procedures are adopted. **The difference is** that when shares that are redeemable are issued it is made quite clear at the point of issued that they will be redeemed. On the other hand, shares issued without this proviso cannot be redeemed. Such shares can be bought back, but there is yet another golden rule, which is that a company cannot buy back all its shares and it must, after the purchase, have other shares in issue which are not redeemable. This is to prevent a company redeeming /purchasing all its shared and with **no members.**

Advantage of purchasing/Redeeming Shares

The main advantage of buying back or redeeming shares for public companies is when there are large cash resource and it may be useful to return some of the surplus cash to the shareholders. This will avoid the pressure put on directors to use in uneconomic ways.

B. DIVIDENDS.

The shareholder of a company gets his reward in the form of a share of the profits and his share is called **a dividend**.

Preference Dividends.

The preference shareholder is one who is entitled to a specific rate of dividend before the ordinary or equity shareholders receive anything. The rate which will be established when the shares are issued and is usually expressed as a percentage of the nominal value, e.g. 10% preference shares, which means that if the shareholder held 100 £1 preference shares he would receive a £10 dividend.

You should note that this type of share has declined and it is now more usual for companies to have a single class of shareholder.

Ordinary Dividends.

Ordinary dividends are paid on ordinary or equity shares and the rate is usually expressed as a percentage, e.g. a 10% dividend on £500,000 ordinary shares will amount to £50,000.

The Act state that:

> "*All dividends shall be declared and paid according to the amounts paid up on shares on which the dividend is paid. A dividend while the company continues in business may be of any size that is recommended by the directors and approved the members.*"

The amount distributed to members is proportional to either the nominal value of the shares held, or the amount paid-up if they are partly paid.

Members may approve a dividend proposed by the directors or they can reject or reduce it, but they **cannot increase** a proposed dividend.

Interim Dividends

Provided the article so authorize and there are, in the opinion of the directors, sufficient fund to warrant paying an interim dividend, then one may be paid. This means that approximately halfway through the financial year, if the company is making sufficient profits, the directors have the authority to pay a dividend. The directors do not require the members to authorize such dividends. The dividends are calculated in the same way as the final proposed dividend after the final accounts have been prepared.

C.DEBENTURES

A debenture is a written acknowledgement of a **loan to a company**, which carries a fixed rate of interest.

Debentures are not part of the capital of a company. Interest payable to debenture holders must be paid as a matter of right and is therefore classified as loan interest, **a financial expense,** in the profit and loans account. A shareholder, on the other hand , is only paid a **dividend o**n his investment if the company makes a profit, and such dividend, if paid, is an **appropriation of profit**.

Type of Debenture

(a) **Simple or Naked Debentures**.
These are debentures for which no security has been arranged as regards to payment of interest or repayment of principal.

(b) **Mortgage or fully Secured Debentures**
Debentures of this type are securities are by a specific mortgage of certain fixed assets of the company.

(c) **Floating Debentures**
Debentures of this type are secured by floating charge on the property of the company. This charge permits the company to deal with any of its assets in the ordinary course of its business, unless and until the charge become fixed or crystallized.

An example should make clear the difference between a mortgage, which is a fixed over some specific asset, and a debenture which is secured by a floating charge. Suppose that a company has factories in London, Manchester and Glasgow. The company may borrow money by issuing debentures with a fixed charge over the Glasgow factory. As long as the loan remains unpaid, the company's use of the Glasgow factory is restricted by the mortgage. The company might wish to sell some of the buildings, but the charge on the property as a whole would be a hindrance.

On the other hand, if it issued floating debentures then there is no charge on any specific part of the assets of the company and, unless and until the company becomes insolvent, there is no restriction on the company acting freely in connection with any of its property.

Rights of Debenture Holders
The rights of debentures holders are:
- They are entitled to payment of interest at the agreed ate.
- They are entitled to be repaid on expiry of the terms of the debenture as fixed by deed.
- In the event of the company failing to pay the interest due to them or should they have reason to suppose that the assets upon which their loan is secured are in jeopardy, they may cause a receiver to be appointed. The receiver has power to sell a company's assets in order to satisfy all claims of the debenture holders.

The differences between shareholders and debenture holders are summarized in the following table:

Debentures Holder	Shareholder
Debentures are not part of the capital of a company.	Shares are part of the capital of a company.
Debentures rank first for capital and interest.	Shares are postponed to the claims of debenture holders and other creditors.
Debenture interest must be paid whether there are profits or not and is a charge to the profit and loss account.	Dividends are payable out of profits only (appropriation)
Debentures are usually secured by a charge on the company's assets.	but only if there is adequate profit.
	Shares cannot carry a charge.
Debentures holders are creditors, not members of the company, and usually have no control over it.	Shareholders are members of the company and have indirect control over its management.

Debentures are not part of capital; therefore, they are not to be included together with the shares in the balance sheet.

Gearing

The gearing of a company is the ratio of fixed-interest and fixed-dividend capital (i.e. debentures plus preference shares) to ordinary (equity) shares capital plus reserves. We will consider this when we look at accounting ratios later, but you should be aware that a company's gearing can have important repercussions, as debenture interest must be paid regardless of profitability.

Issues at par and at a Discount

Where as shares **may not** be issued at a discount, debentures may. This means that the lender pays less than the nominal valve.

(a) Issues at Par
    This is the same as issuing shares at par, i.e. a £100 debenture would raise £100.
(b) Issues at a Discount

This means that the value raised by the issue is less than the par value, e.g. a £100 debenture would raise in cash, say, £80. This discount can be deducted from the shares premium account. The entries in the accounts would look like this:

	£	£
Cash		80
Share premium account *		20
Debenture		100

- Clearly there would be a balance in the account. This illustration merely shows the basic entries.

As you see, the debenture will appear in the accounts at its full value. You may wonder why a company would take this step and there is no mystery; it is just a ploy to encourage the public invest.

Redemption of Debentures

As debentures can be issued at par or at a discount they can also be redeemed at a value greater than that paid, e.g. if you pay £80 then the redemption value is quite likely to be £100 and if you pay the par value of £100 then you might well get £120 back. Again the difference –if any –can be written off to the share premium account.

There are three ways of financial redemption of debentures:

- Out of the proceeds of a new issue of shares or debentures.
- Out of the balance on the profits and loss account and existing resource of the business (cash).
- Out of a sinking fund built up over the years with or without investments (the investment really being a savings fund).

When shares are redeemed or purchased there is a statutory requirement to make a transfer to the capital redemption reserve. The reason for this is because shares are part of the capital of the company where as debentures are merely long-term liabilities or loans.

Restrictions on Borrowings.

Restriction on borrowings outstanding at any time may be contained in the articles of association of the company, imposed by resolution of shareholders, or included in the loan agreement or trust deed.

D. TYPES AND SOUCES S OF FINANCE.

Balancing Fixed and Working capital

The assets of a business are financed by its liabilities, as shown in the balance sheet. Every business need:

- Fixed capital-to finance fixed assets.
- Working capital-to finance current assets.

Ultimately, all business must be supported by the long-term capital base, but short-term borrowings may be used to cover temporary lulls in trade in order to maintain the return on capital employed.

Working capital-stocks, debtors and cash-must be carefully managed so that it is adequate but not excessive.

Types of Business and Capital Structure

The types of business organization influence the capital structure. In a small business the financial structure tends to be relatively straightforward. On the other hand, with the large public company an extremely complicated capital structure may be present.

(a) Sole Trader and Partnership
With the sole trader or partnership, the initial fund generally comes from the owners themselves. Any extra requirements for the seasonal needs or other purposes may be obtained from a bank. Remember also that credit purchases are a very important form of financing.

The fixed assets of the sole trader's business or the partnership may be obtained by leasing or by hire purchase; all that the owner of the business has to do is to establish a good credit standing.

With this type of small business, great care must be taken to ensure that overtrading does not occur. Overtrading is when there is a high turnover, requiring more stock and higher costs, with an insufficient capital base to support it. There is great danger of overtdading when too much finance is obtained through hire purchase or the leasing of premises or other fixed assets. Payments have to be made in the form of interest or similar charges, and these are fixed charges which have to be covered whether the business makes a profit or not.

(b) Private Limited Company
The private company requires great cash resources and, when finance from the owners is inadequate, additional cash must be obtained from external sources. The constraint here is that shares cannot be offered to the general public.

(c) Public limited Company
The public company can obtain funds through the issue of shares to the general public.

In determining the types of funds to be raised, every business must consider the reasons for needing these funds and the use to which they will be put. For example, it is not likely that share capital would be raised to solve a short-term liquidity problem.

Long-term funds

(a) Owner's Capital
This is the amount contributed by the owner(s) of a business, and it is supplemented by retained profit.

In the case of a limited company, a great many individuals can own shares in the company. There are two main types of shares-ordinary shares and preference shares, as we have seen. The decision about the proportions of ordinary shares and preferences shares (if any) to issue is not an easy one, and will be influenced by the type of company, as well as by other factors.

(b) loans
There are a number of forms of long-term loan available to a business:

- *Unsecured Loan*

This is an advance for a specified sum which is repaid at a future agreed date. Interest is charged per annum on the total amount of the loan or on the amount outstanding.

- *Secured Loans*

These tend to for larger amounts over larger periods. Security is required in the form of a specified asset or it is spread over all assets of the business (a "floating" change). If the borrower defaults on the loan, on the lender is allowed to dispose of the secured asset (s) to recover the amount owed to him. Since there is less risk to the lender, secured loans are cheaper than unsecured ones.

- *Mortgage Loans*

These are specific secured loans for the purchase of an asset, the asset itself giving security to the lender – e.g. purchase of premises.

- *Debentures*

These, as we have seen, are a special type of company loan, broken into small-value units to allow transferability. They carry a fixed rate of interest which is a charge against profits and to be paid irrespective of the level of profits.

Note that loan interest is a charge against profits and it is, therefore, allowed for tax proposes, unlike dividends on shares.

(c) Venture Capital

Obtaining finance to start up a new business can be very difficult. Venture capital is finance provided by (an) investors (s) who is (are) willing to take a risk that the new company will be succeful. Usually, a business proposal plan will need to be submitted to the venture capitalist, so that the likely success of the business can be assessed.

(d) Leasing (longer-term)

This source of funds has grown substantially in recent years, and it is an important method of funding the acquisition of fixed assets. The business selects its required asset and the leasing Company purchases it. Then the business uses the asset and pays the leasing company a rent. The payments are regular (e.g. month) and for fixed amounts.

A development of leasing is a process called **sale and leaseback**, in which the assets owned and used by a business are sold to a leasing company and then rented back over a long period. The cash proceeds from the sale provide immediate funds for business use.

Lease purchase agreements are also possible, where part of the fixed monthly payment goes towards the purchase of the asset and part is a rental cost.

(e) Hire Purchase (longer-term)

This is very similar to leasing, although the ultimate objective, in this case, is for the business to acquire title to the asset when the final hire-purchase payment is made. The business can thus claim capital allowances on such assets, which reduce its tax liability.

Shorter-term Funds

(a) Trade Credit

Trade credit it is a significant source of funds for most business, because payment can be made after the receipt of goods/services. However, a balance must be achieved between using trade credit for funding and the problem of loss of supplier good will if payments are regularly late.

(b) Overdrafts

Here a bank allows the business to overdraw on its account up to certain level. This is a very common for of short-term finance.

(c) Grants (these can be for long-term purposes)

Grants are mainly provided by the government and its agencies. They include grants for special project, e.g. energy-conservation grants for specific industries, such as mining, and grants for specific geographical areas.

(d) Leasing and Hire Purchase

These can also be arranged on a short-term basis

(e) Factoring

This is a service provided to a business which increases its liquidity. The factoring organization will, for a fee, take over the accounts section of its client and send out invoices and collect money from debtors. It also provides a service where by the client may receive up to say, 80% of the value of a sales invoice as soon as it is sent to the customer and the remaining money is passed on when collected by the factor.

The problem with this method is that factors are very careful about accepting clients, and they reject many organizations which approach them. Also, some personal contact with customers is lost, which can harm trade.

Interest Rate Exposure

When considering a loan or other financial arrangement, the benefits deriving from what that borrowing finances will be set against its forecast costs. If the economic situation changes and the difference between costs and benefits is squeezed (say by increased costs of financing) the company will become less profitable. The general level of interest rates is a very important factor in financial planning.

Sources of External Finance

Having looked at the various types of finance available, let's now consider the organizations which provide or help provide funds.

(a)Clearing Banks.

These play a vital part in the provision of funds, particularly to small business. They provide:

- Overdrafts
- Personal loans-unsecured
- Personal loans-secured
- Medium-term loans – designed to help businesses to expand and develop. Often, repayments can be tailored to suit the individual borrower.

(b) Merchant Banks

These provide development capital but they are very selective in the organization they choose to help. Nominally the bankers require, as security, a seat on the board of directors and active involvement in the management of the company. Development purposes include expansion, buying out partners, product development, and overcoming tax problems.

(c) Specialist Instructions

There are a number of specialist instructions – e.g. group (Investors in Industry) – which provide finance, particularly for new business start-ups or management buyouts.

(d) Foreign Banks
These account for about 30% of all bank advances to UK manufacturing industries. They are often slightly cheaper than clearing bank loans. Foreign banks are unlikely to lend below £50,000.

(e) Insurance Companies.
These can use for obtaining mortgage facilities on the purchase of property.

(f) Pension Funds
Several pension funds have invested in company projects.

(g) Share Issues thought the Stock Exchange.
Companies wishing to raise funds through a public issue of shares invariably use the services of an issuing house. These are experts in new issues and they provide administrative support and advice.

(h) Local Authorities
These have certain powers to provide assistance to industry where this would benefit the local area. Finance is usually in the form of loans, improvement grants or factory space.

(i) Central Government and the Europe
There are number of different fields in which assistance is provide from these sources – e.g. regional aid, tax relief for investing in new companies.

Examples of Business Financing

The following is the balance sheet of newly opened corner shop/general store. Do you feel that the fixed and working capital has correctly balanced? Comment on any different approach that you might like to see as regards financing.

Balance Sheet as at ……………………

	£	£
Fixed Assets		
Land buildings		350,000
Fittings		5,000
Current Assets		
Stock	1, 000	
Cash	500	
	1,500	
Current liabilities		
Bank overdraft	5,000	
Trade creditors	1,000	
	6,000	
		(4,500)
		35,500
Long-term Liabilities		
Mortgage loan		30,000
		5,500
Capital		5,500

This example is somewhat "larger than life" in that it is most unlikely that such a venture would be financed.

Fixed and working capital has not been well balanced at all. It seems that stock has been purchased entirely on credit and that it is at a very low level. Unless another delivery is expected shortly it seems unlikely that £1,000 stock would satisfy customers for very long. In addition, the bank overdraft seems to be financing fixed assets (fittings). This is a mismatch of short-and long-term and is poor financing.

As to the remainder of the financing, much of the land and buildings appears to be under mortgage, with a very small capital contribution from the owners.

The venture looks doomed from the beginning. Think about the level of profit needed to meet interest charges alone on this level of borrowing-without considering repayment.

E. MANAGEMENT OF WORKING CAPITAL

Working Capital Cycle

Working capital is **current assets less current liabilities**.

When a business begins to operate, cash will initially be provided by the proprietor or shareholders. This cash is then used to purchase fixed assets, with part being held to buy inventories of materials and to pay employees` wages. This finances the setting-up-of the business to produce goods/service to sell to customers for cash, which sooner or later is received back by the business and used to purchase further materials, pay wages, etc,and so the process is repeated.

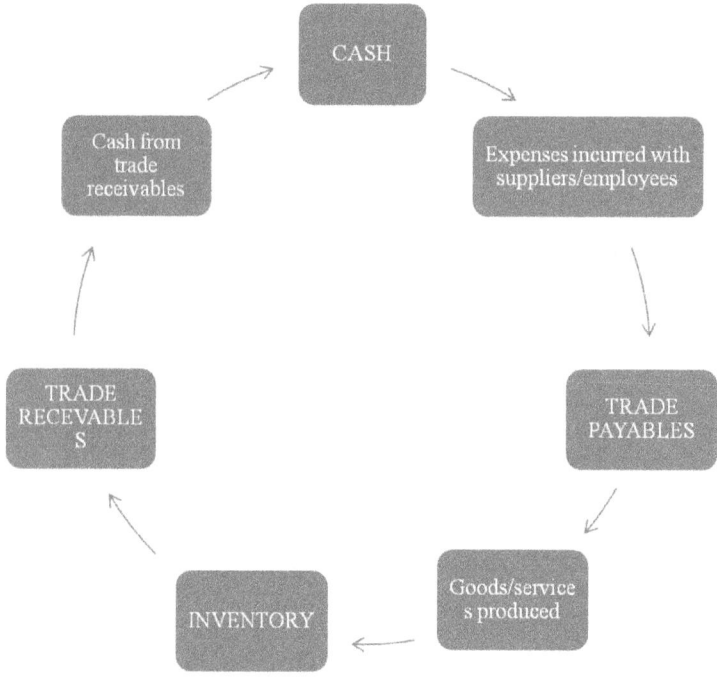

Problems arise when, at any given time in time in the business cycle, there is insufficient cash to pay trade payables, which could have the business placed in liquidation if payment of debits is not received. An alternative would be for the business to borrow to overcome the cash shortage, but this can be in terms of interest payments, even if a bank is prepared to grant a loan.

Striking the Right Balance

Working capital requirements can fluctuate because of seasonal business variations, interruption to normal trading conditions, or government influences,e.g. changes in interest or tax rates. Unless the business has sufficient working capital available to cope with these fluctuations, expensive loans become necessary; otherwise insolvency may result. On the other hand, the situation may arise where a business has too much working capital tied up in idle inventories or with large trade receivable which could lose interest and therefore reduce profits.

Irrespective of the method used for financing fixed current assets, it ids extremely important to ensure that there is **sufficient** working capital at all times but that this is **not excessive**. If working capital is in short supply, the fixed assets cannot be employed as effectively as is required to earn maximum profits. Conversely, if the working capital is too high, too much money is being locked up in inventories and other current assets. Possibly, the excessive working capital will have been built up at the sacrifice of fixed assets. If this is so, there will be a tendency for low efficiency to persist, with the inevitable running down of profits.

The management of working capital is extremely important function in a business. It is mainly a balancing process between the cost of holding current assets and the risks associated with holding very small or zero amounts of them.

(a) Management of Inventories

Inventories may include raw materials, work in progress and/ or finished goods. The balance to be struck here is between holding or not holding inventories.

(j) The cost of holding inventories

These include:
- Financing costs – the costs of producing funds to acquired the inventory held
- Storage costs
- Insurance costs
- Cost of losses because of theft, damage, etc.
- Obsolescence cost and deterioration costs

These costs can be considerable, and estimates suggest they can be between 20% and 100% per annum of the value of the inventory held.

(ii) The cost of holding very low (r zero) inventories
These include

- Cost of loss of customer goodwill if inventories not available

- Ordering costs – low inventory levels are usually associated with higher ordering costs than are bulk purchases

- Cost of production hold-ups owing to insufficient inventories

The organization will set the balance, which achieves the minimum total cost, and arrive at optimal inventory levels.

(b) Management of Trade Receivables

The management of trade receivables requires identification and balancing of the following costs:

(i) Costs of allowing credit

These include:

- Financing costs
- Cost of maintaining trade receivables' accounting records
- Cost of collecting the debts
- Cost of bad debts written of
- Cost of obtaining a credit reference
- Inflation cost – outstanding debts in periods of high inflation will lose value

(ii) Costs of refusing credit

These include:

- Loss of customer goodwill
- Security costs owing to increased cash collection

Again, the organization will attempt to balance the two categories of costs – although this is not an easy task, as costs are often difficult to quantify. It is normal practice to establish credit limits for individual trade receivables.

(c) Management of Cash

Again, two categories of cost need to be balanced:

(i) Costs of holding cash

These include

- Loss of interest if cash were invested
- Loss of purchasing power during times of high inflation
- Security and insurance costs

(ii) Costs of not holding cash

These include:

- Cost of inability to meet bills as they fall due
- Cost of lost opportunities for special-offer purchases
- Cost of borrowing to obtain cash to meet unexpected demands

Once again, the organization must balance these cost to arrive at an optimal level of cash to hold. The technique of cash budgeting is of great help in cash management.

F. The Nature of a Balance Sheet
    Difference between Trial Balance and Balance Sheet
    Function of the Balance Sheet
    Summarized Statement

G. Assets and Liabilities in the Balance Sheet
    Type of asset
    Valuation of Assets
    Order of Assets in the Balance Sheet
    Liabilities to proprietors
    External Liabilities

H. Distinction between Capital and Revenue
    Definitions
    Capital and Revenue Receipts

I. Preparation of Balance Sheet
    Sole Trader
    Partnership

Answers to Questions for Practice

INTRODUCTION

Every business, sooner or later, wants to know the result of its trading, i.e. whether a profit has been made or a loss sustained, and whether it is still financially solvent. For this reason, the following accounts must be prepared at the end of the year (or at intervals during the year if the business so chooses):

(a) Manufacturing Account
This applies only to a manufacturing business, and shows the various costs of producing the goods.

(b) Trading Account
The purpose of this account is to calculate the **gross profit** of a trading business, and this is done by showing the revenue from the sale of goods, and the cost of acquiring those goods.

(c) Profit and Loss Account (Statement of Comprehensive Income or Earnings)
A business has many expenses not directly related to manufacturing or trading activities, and these are shown in the profit and loss account. By subtracting them from gross profit, a figure for **net profit** (or loss) is found. A business selling a service will produce just a profit and loss account.

(d) Appropriation Account
A business now has to decide what to do with its net profit. The way in which this profit is distributed (or "appropriate") is shown in the appropriation account. This account is not used in the case of a sole trader, the net profit being transferred to the proprietor's capital account.

(e) Balance Sheet (Statement of Financial Position)
This is a statement of the assets owned by the business, and the liabilities outstanding. It is not strictly an account.

So you can see that we arrive at the results of a firm's trading in two stages. Firstly, from the manufacturing and trading accounts we ascertain gross profit. Secondly, from the profit and loss account we determine net profit. You will often see the manufacturing, trading and profit and loss accounts presented together and headed simply "income statement for the year ending….."

A. THE TRIAL BALANCE

Before drawing up the final accounts and the balance sheet, it is usual to prepare a list of all the balances in the accounts ledger. This is known as the **trial balance**.

Each account in the firm's books is balanced off. This means adding up the debit and credit sides and then comparing the totals. If for example, the debit side adds up to £500 and the credit side to £400, then the lesser figure is deducted from the greater figure, and the difference would be shown as a debit balance and entered into the trial balance (in this case it would amount to £100).

Having drawn up the trial balance, and proving that the two sides have similar totals; it is then possible to begin to draw up the final accounts. Remember that even if the trial balance has similar amounts on both the debit and credit totals, this only proves the **arithmetical accuracy** of the entries in the ledger accounts.

A Typical Balance (Sole Trader)

	Debit £	Credit £
Capital		84,000
Drawing	10,000	
Trade receivables	20,000	
Trade payables		7,000
Provision for doubtful debts		700
Non-current assets at cost	60,000	
Depreciation of non-current assets		19,000
Inventory (trading)	32,000	
Telephone expenses	3,000	
Sundries	1,000	
Cash in hand/bank	1,900	
Purchases trading inventory	55,000	
Sales		17,000
Wages	35,000	
Insurance	1,600	
Audit	3,000	
Motor vehicle expenses	9,000	
Rent	9,000	
Salaries (office)	12,000	
Office cleaning	9,000	
Carriage inwards	2,200	
Advertising	5,000	
Commissions paid	7,000	
Loss on canteen	5,000	
	280,700	280,700

Note: this model is provided to give you an idea of the layout and of some of the typical items that may be included in a trial balance. There is no need to try and learn where all the items can be found.

B.TRADING ACCOUNT

For the sake of simplicity, we will assume here that the business purchase ready-goods and resells them a profit.

What is gross profit? If it purchase quantity of seeds for £15, I have made a gross profit of £5. In the trading account we have to collect all those items which are directly concerned with the cost or selling price of the goods in which we trade.

Layout

The main items in the trading account are shown in the following model layout. Carriage inwards, i.e. on purchases, and customers duties on purchases, etc. are expense incidental to the acquisition b y the business of the goods which are intended for resale, and are therefore debited to the trading account.

	£	£	£
Sales			xxxx
less sales returns (Returns inwards)			xxxx
Turnover			xxxx
Cost of goods sold:			
Opening inventory		xxxx	
Purchase	xxxx		
less Returns (Returns outwards)	xxxx		
	xxxx		
add Carriage inwards	xxxx		
		xxxx	
		xxxx	
less closing inventory		xxxx	xxxx
Gross profit (loss)			xxxx

Note how sales returns are deducted from sales, and purchases returns from purchases.

Gross profit may be defined as the excess of the setting price of goods over their cost price, due allowance being made for opening and closing inventories, and for costs incidental in getting the goods into ....valuation of inventories in a later study unit

Example

From the following balances extracted from the books of TUKUNYEMA Co. Ltd, prepare a trading account for the year ended 31 December:

Balances at 31 December Year 1

	Dr	Cr
	£	£
Purchases	140,251	
Sales		242,761
Purchases returns		4,361
Sales returns	9,471	
Inventory as at 1 January	54,319	
Customs and landing charges (re purchases)	2,471	
Carriage inwards	4,391	

Inventory in hand at 31 December was valued at £64,971.

NB These are not all the balances in the books of the company – only those necessary for compiling the trading account.

As you know that all these items are trading account items, this makes the exercise easy, but remember that in practice the accountant will have to select, out of the various items in the trial balance, those which are trading account items.

TUKUNYEMA Co. Ltd
Trading Account for year ended 31 December…

	£	£	£
Sales	242,761		
Less Sales returns		9,471	
233,290			
Cost of goods sold:			
Opening stock		54,319	
Purchases	140,251		
Less returns outwards		4,361	
	135,890		
Customs and landing charges	2,471		
Carriage inwards	4,391	142,752	
		197,071	
Less Closing inventory		64,971	132,100
Gross profit			**101,190**

B. TRADING ACCOUNT

For the sake of simplicity, we will assume here that the business purchases ready-made goods and resells them at a profit.

What is gross profit? If I purchase a quantity of seeds for £10 and sell them for £15, I have made a gross profit of £5. In the trading account we have to collect all those items which are directly concerned with the cost or selling price of the goods in which we trade.

Layout
The main items in the trading account are shown in the following model layout. Carriage inwards, i.e. on purchases, and customs duties on purchase, etc. are expenses incidental to the acquisition by the business of the goods which are intended for resale, and are therefore debited to the trading account.

	£	£	£
Sales			xxxx
Less sales returns (Returns inwards)			xxxx
Turnover			xxxx
Cost of goods sold:			
Opening inventory		xxxx	
Purchases	xxxx		
Less Returns (Returns outwards)	xxxx		
	xxxx		
add Carriage inwards	xxxx		
		xxxx	
		xxxx	
less Closing inventory		xxxx	xxxx
Gross profit (loss)			**xxxx**

Note how sales returns are deducted from sales, and purchases returns from purchases.
Gross profit may be defined as the excess of the selling price of goods over their cost price, due allowance being made for opining and closing inventories, and for costs incidental in getting the goods into their present condition and location. We will look at the valuation of inventories in a later study unit.

Questions for practice
1.   (a) From the following balances extracted from the ledger of Wajanja & Co. on
       31 October, prepare the trading account of the business for the year ended 31 October

Purchases	£24,720
Sales	£40,830
Purchases returns	£1,230
Sales returns	£1,460
Carriage inwards	£2,480
Inventory as at 1 November (i.e. beginning of year)	£6,720
Inventory at end of year	£7,630

   (c) In what way would the trading account of Wajanja & Co. be different if the proprietor,
      Mr. Wajanja, had withdrawn goods for his own use valued at £500 selling price?
Now check your answers with those provided at the end of the unit.

B.   MANUFACTURING ACCOUNT

In dealing with our trading account, we have assumed that the business purchase finished articles and resold them in the same condition, without making any alteration to them. Such a business is a trading concern only. As you know, many businesses do more than this. They purchase raw materials and convert them into finished articles by a process of manufacture. Manufacture involves a number of factors, each contributing its own measure of cost to the final product when it is ready for the market. A simple trading account would not be appropriate for the purpose of dealing with these various expenses, so we use a manufacturing account.

The primary purpose of the manufacturing account is to arrive at the cost of production of the articles produced within a given period. A secondary purpose may be that of arriving at a theoretical profit on manufacturing (manufacturing profit)

The cost of production comprises such factors as raw materials, manufacturing wages, carriage inwards, factory power and fuel, factory rent, rates, insurance, etc. the expenses must not be debited to the manufacturing account haphazardly; the layout and sequence of this account is important.

Layout
The account is built up by stages:
  (a) **Cost of materials used** – i.e. opening inventory of raw materials plus purchase of raw materials less closing inventory of raw materials.
  (b) Carriage inwards, duty, freight, etc. will be added to purchases, while purchases returns will be deducted. The purchases figure will be after deduction of trade discount.
  (c) **Direct labour costs-** i.e. wages paid to workmen engaged on actual production.
  (d) **Direct expenses-**which are any expenses incurred on **actual production**.
  (e) **Prime cost-**i.e. the sub-total of (a),(b),(c) and (d).
  (f) **Factory overheads or indirect expenses** associated with production such as factory rent and rates, salary of works manager, and depreciation of plant, machinery and factory buildings.
  (g) Work in progress at the beginning of the period (added)
  (h) Work in progress at the end of period (deducted)
  (i) **Cost of production-**i.e. adjusted total of (g) and (h)

Sol in outline the layout is:

Direct materials

Direct labour

Direct expenses

PRIME COST

Factory overheads or Indirect
Expenses

TOTOAL PRODUCTION COST

Example

The following is an extract from a trial balance

	£	£
Opening inventory of raw materials	90,000	
Opening inventory of work in progress	75,000	
Returns out wards-raw materials		2,500
Purchases-raw materials	160,000	
Wages direct	83,000	
Wages indirect	65,000	
Expenses direct	22,000	
Carriage inwards-raw materials	7,900	
Rent factory	25,000	
Fuel and power	17,370	
General factory expenses	32,910	
Opening inventory-finished goods	97,880	
Sales		548,850

The closing inventories are:

Raw materials   £74,000

Work in progress   £68,000

Finished goods   £83,500

We can prepare the manufacturing and trading accounts together as follows:

Manufacturing and Trading Account for ………..

	£	£
Opening inventory of raw materials		90,000
Purchases raw materials	160,000	
Less Returns outwards	(2,5000)	
	157,500	
Carriage inwards	(7,900)	165,400
		255,400
Less closing inventory of raw materials		(74,000)
Total cost of raw materials		181,400
Direct wages	83,000	
Direct expenses	22,000	105,000
Prime cost		286,400
Indirect expenses:		
Wages	65,000	
Fuel and power	17,370	
General factory expenses	32,910	
Rent	25,000	140,280
		426,680
Opening WP		75,000
		501,680

Less closing WP		(68,000)
Total cost of production		433,680
Sales		548,850
Opening inventory finished goods	97,880	
Production costs	433,680	
	531,560	
Less closing inventory finished goods	(83,500)	(448,060)
Gross trading profit		**100,790**

C.   PROFIT AND LOSS ACCOUNT

No business can function without incurring what are known as overhead expenses. For example, there are salaries, rent, stationery and other incidentals which must be met out of the gross profit made. In addition, a business may earn a small income quite a part from the gross profit, e.g. dividends and interest on investments.

The purpose of the profit and loss account is to gather all the revenue credits and debits of the business (other than those dealt with in the manufacturing and/or trading account)so that it can be seen whether a net profit has been earned or a net loss incurred for the period covered by the account.

Credits

The items appearing as credit in the profit and loss account include:

- Gross profit on trading – brought from the trading account.
- Discounts received.
- Rents received in respect of property let. (If rents are received from the subletting of part of the factory premises, the rent of which is debited to the manufacturing account, then these should be credited to manufacturing account. In effect this reduces the rent debit to that applicable to the portion of the factory premises actually occupied by the business.)
- Interest and dividends received in respect of investments owned by business.
- Bad debits recovered.
- Other items of profit or gain, other than of a capital nature, including profits on the sale of assets.

Debits.

All the overhead expenses of the business: - are debited to the profit and loss account. Items entered as debits in the profit and loss account should be arranged in a logical and recognizable order. The following subdivisions of overhead expenses indicate one recommended order (although this is not the only order in use).

(a) Administration Expenses

These cover rent, rates, lighting, heating and repairs etc. of office buildings, directors` remuneration and fees, salaries of managers and clerks, office expenses of various types. In general, all the expenses incurred in the **control** of the business and the direction and formulation of its policy.

(b) Sales Expenses

Included in these are travelers` commission, salaries of sales staff, warehouse rent, rates and expenses in respect of the warehouse, advertising and any expenses connected with the selling of the goods dealt in, e.g. bad debits

(c) Distribution Expenses

Here we have cost of carriage outwards. (Remember that carriage inwards, i.e. on purchases is debited to the trading account; it is not really an overhead charge as it increases the cost of the purchase.) Under this heading we also have such items as freight (where goods are sold to customers abroad), expenses of motor vans and wages of the drivers, wages of packers and any other expenses incurred by the **distribution** or delivery of the goods dealt in.

(d) Financial Expenses

These include bank charges, interest on loans, hire purchase agreements, debentures, mortgages, bank overdrafts, etc.

No capital expense items must be debited to profit and loss account. This is extremely important. An example of a capital item is the purchase of plant and machinery by a manufacturing business.

Items Requiring Special Attention

There are several items which do not occur in the normal course of business but which must be carefully considered at the end of each trading period.

(a) Bad Debits

If all the trade receivable of a firm paid their accounts, no mention of this item would be made. Unfortunately, however, they do bit, and many firms incur what are known as bad debit. For instance, where a debtor is declared a bankrupt, the whole of his debit will not be settled. Only a part of it is paid, but as far as the law is concerned, the debit is wiped out. Consequently, the unsettled portion of the debit is of no value, and it must be written off as a loss. Similarly, if trade receivables disappear, or if their debits are not worth the trouble of court action, the debits must be written off.

The debtor's account is credited with the amount of debt, thus closing the account. To complete the double entry, the debts account is debited. All bad debts incurred during the trading period are debited to the bad debts account.

At the end of the trading period the bad debts account is credited with the total bad debts, to close the account. The double entry is preserved by debiting profit and loss account with the same amount.

Bad debts are sometimes considered to be a financial expense, for they arise from the financial policy of selling goods on credit rather than for cash. However, they are more appropriately classified as a sales expense, as they result directly from sales.

(b) Bank Charges
These are charges made by the form's bank for working the account of the firm, and are therefore debited to profit and loss account. Bank charges are financial expense.

(c) Debenture Interest
As debenture holders are trade payable of the company, their interest must be paid whether the company is able to show a profit or not. Therefore it is an expense and, as such must be debited to profit and loss account.
Remember the difference between debenture interest and dividends paid. The former is interest on an outside loan whilst the latter is merely distribution of profit.

(d) Depreciation

Assets such as plant and machinery, warehouse or factory buildings, delivery vehicle, are used directly in the manufacture of goods or in trading and, as a result of this, their value must decrease owing to wear and tear. This decrease in value must be allowed for when overhead charges are being debited to the manufacturing, trading or profit and loss account. We will look at how to estimate the amount to charge each year for depreciation in a later study unit.
Each year the depreciation account will increase in value, until the balance on that account equals the cost price shown in the asset account. At this point, no further depreciation should be charge to the profit and loss account.
Depreciation of such asset as office furniture must also be allowed for in profit and loss account. Where, however, there is a manufacturing account, the depreciation of all assets which are actually engaged in production, e.g. plant and machinery, should be recorded in it, because such depreciation is a manufacturing expense. Normally the depreciation provision is the last charge to be shown in the both the manufacturing account and the profit and loss account.

Where there is a profit or loss on the disposal of a fixed asset, this is shown in the profit and loss account immediately after the expense of depreciation.

(e) Discount

There are usually two discount accounts, one for discounts received and one for discounts allowed. The former is a credit balance and the latter a debit balance. At the end of the trading period, discounts received account is debited and profit and loss account credited, as item under this heading are benefits received by the firm. Discounts allowed account is credited and profit and loss account debited, as these items are expense of the firm. Discounts allowed can be classified as a financial expense but are more usually shown as a separate item in the profit and loss account.

(f) Dividends Paid (Limited Company Only)

This item, which will appear as a debit balance in the trial balance, represents profits which have been distributed amongst the shareholders of the company. It is not therefore an expense of the company and must **not** be debited to the profit and loss account,. This item must be debited to the approbation account (see later). If no profits have been made. No dividends will be paid to shareholders.

(g) Drawings (Partnership or Trader)

The drawings of a partner or sale trader are not expense of the business and must not therefore, be debited to the profit and loss account. Drawings are the withdrawals of cash or goods service from the business by the partner or sole trader.

(h) Goodwill

This is an item which often appears as an asset of a business. It is the value attached to the probability that old customers will continue to patronize the firm. Thus, where a company purchases another business, it may pay £500,000 for assets which are agreed as being worth only £450,000. The difference of £50,000 will be the value of the goodwill.

In such circumstances, the company might decide to write off the goodwill over a number of years, say ten years say ten years. In this case the profit or loss account would be debited annually with £5,000 and goodwill account credited, until the later account ceases to exist. Often, however, the firm decides to write off the entire amount of any goodwill immediately.

(i) Preliminary Expenses (Limited Company Only)

These are expenses incurred at the time a limited company is set up, and consist chiefly of legal charges connected with the incorporation of the company. Under the Companies Act they be written off immediately.

(j) Provision for Bad Debts

In addition to writing off bad debts as they occur or when they are known to be bad, a business should also provide for any losses it may incur in the future as a result of its present trade receivables being unable to meet their obligations. If a business has book debts totaling £100,000, it is not very likely that all those trade receivables will pay their account in full. Some of the debts may prove to be bad, but this may not be known for some considerable time.

The amount of the provision should be determined by a careful examination of the list of trade receivables at the balance sheet date. If any of these debits are bad, they should be written off at once. If any debts are doubtful, it should be estimated how much the debtor is likely to pay. The balance of his debt is potentially bad, and the provision should be the total of such potentially bad amounts. The debtor`s account will not, however, be written off until it is definitely known that it is bad.

The provision is formed for the purpose of reducing the values of trade receivables 0n the balance sheet to an amount which it is expected will be received from them. It is **not** an estimate of the bad debits which will arise in the succeeding period. Bad debits arising in the next period will result from credit sales made within that period as well as from debit outstanding at the beginning of the period. It is therefore quite incorrect to debit bad debts against the provision for bad debts. Once the latter account has been opened, the only alteration in it is that required to increase or decrease its balance – by debit or credit to profit and loss account. This alteration is included as a financial expense when a debit.

(**Never** show provision for bad debts with the liabilities on the balance sheet – it is always deducted from the amount of trade receivables under the assets on the balance sheet – sees later.)

(k) Provision for Discounts Allowable

If a business allows discount to its customers for prompt payment, it is likely that some of the trade receivables at the balance sheet date will actually pay less than the full amount of their debt. To include trade receivables at the face value of such debts, without providing for discounts which may be claimed, is to overstate the financial position of the business. So, a provision for discounts allowable should be made by debt to profit and loss account. If made on a percentage basis, it should be reckoned in relation to potentially good debts, i.e. trade receivables less provision for bad debts, for if it is thought that a debt is sufficiently doubtful for a provision to be raised against it, it is hardly likely that debtor will pay his account promptly and claim discount.

The provision appears as a deduction in the balance sheet from trade receivables (after the provision for bad debts has been deducted). It is a financial expense.

(l) Expenses Paid in Advance or Arrears (Prepayments and Accruals)

Where are a proportion of expenses, such as rent has been **paid in advance (prepaid)**, this must be allowed for when the profit and loss account is drawn up. For instance, if the firm paid £10,000 rent for six months from 1 November, and the profit and loss account is made out for the year ended 31 December, it would obviously be wrong to debit the profit and loss account with the full amount of £3,333.30 and the other four months` rent,i.e. £6,666.70, should be carried forward and shown in the balance sheet as asset, "Rent paid in advance". These remarks apply equally to any other sum paid in advance, e.g. rates, insurance premiums.

On the other hand, it is often the case that a firm, at the trading period, has incurred expenses which have **not yet been paid** (i.e. have **accrued**). For instance where rent is not payable in advance, a proportion of the rent for the period may be owing when the profit and loss account is drawn up. How is this to be accounted for?

Obviously, profit and loss account will be debited with rent already paid, and it must also be debited with that proportion of the rent which is due but unpaid. Having debited profit and loss account with this latter proportion, we must credit rent account with it. The rent account will then show a credit balance and this must appear as a liability on the balance sheet – it is a debt owing by the business. Then, when this proportion of owing is paid, cash will be credited and rent account debited.

The treatment of expenses (or income) paid or received in advance or in arrears is an example of the accruals concept referred in the course.

Example
The following balances remain in Mkalimoto Juakali`s books after preparation of his trading account for the year ended 30 June:

	Dr £	Cr £
Capital		80,000
Gross profit		10,000
Rates	700	
Insurance	350	
Postage and stationery	270	
Drawings	6,000	
Electricity	800	

The following notes were available at 30 June:

Rates paid in advance	£140
Insurance paid in advance	£250
Electricity account due but unpaid	£170

Prepare Mkalimoto Juakali`s profit and loss account for year ended 30 June.

This would be as follows:

Mkalimoto Juakali

Profit and loss account for the year ended 30 June

	£	£
Gross profit		10,000
less Expenses:		
Rates (700-140)	560	
Insurance (350 – 150)	200	
Postage and stationery	270	
Electricity (800+170)	970	2,000
Net profit		8,000

D. ALLOCATION OR APPROPRIATION OF NET PROFIT

The profit of a business for any period is the excess of its income (gains and profits) over its expenses and losses. It is quite easily ascertained by deducting the total of the debit items in the profit and loss account from the total of the credit items.

We must now consider how the debit to the profit and loss account for net profit (or credit for net loss) is represented by double entry in the books of the business. This differs according to the type of ownership of the business.

The three main types of ownership are sole trader, partnership and limited company, and we shall consider the question of net profit in relation to each in turn.

Sole Trader

This is the simplest case of all (illustrated in the previous example) because the net profit, which is debited to profit and loss account, is credited to the capital account of the sole trader. The trader may have with drawn certain amounts during the trading period; the total of the drawings accounts will then be debited to capital account at the end of the trading period.

Partnership

The allocation net profit (or loss) in the case of a partnership is not quite as simple. When the partnership commences, a document is usually drawn up setting out the rights and duties of all the partners, the amounts of capital to be contributed by each, and the way in which the net profit or loss is to be shared amongst them.

In the case of partnership, the profit and loss account is really in two sections. The first section is drawn up as we have seen in this study unit and is debited with the net profit made (or credited with the ne loss). The second section shows how the net profit is allocated to the various partners, and it is referred to as a **profit and loss appropriation account.**

In a partnership, the partners each have two accounts, the capital account (which is kept intact) and the **current account**. A partner's current is debited with his drawings, and with his proportion of any loss which the business might sustain. It is credited with the partner's share of the net profit and with interest on his capital if this is provided for in the partnership agreement. Thus the capital account of a partner will remain constant, but his current account will fluctuate year by year.

So the appropriation account is credited with the net profit of the trading period. It is debited with any interest on the partners' capitals, where this is provided for in the partnership agreement, and with any salaries.

Then, when these items have been debited, remaining profit can be divided. The appropriation account will be debited with the shares of the remaining profit which are due to the partners. This will close the profit and loss account, and, to complete the double entry, the current account of each partner must be credited with his share of the profit.

Example

Gama, Koba and Mkude are partners who share profits in the proportion of their capitals. Their capitals are £50,000, £20,000 and £10,000 respectively. The net profit for the year before providing for this, or for the following items, is £71,000. Interest on capital is to be allowed at 5 per cent per annum, Mkude is to have a partnership salary of £3,000 per annum. Show how the profit of £71,000 is allocated.

Profit and loss Appropriation Account for year ended 31 December ………..

	£	£
Net profit b/d		71,000
Mkude – salary		3,000
Interest on capital at 5%		
Gama	2,500	
Koba	1,000	
Mkude	500	4,000
Share o profit:		
Gama (5/8)	40,000	
Koba (1/4)	16,000	
Mkude (1/8)	8,000	64,000
		71,000

Thus:	£
Gama`s current account will be credited with (£2,500+£40,000)	42,500
Koba`s current account will be credited with (£1,000+£16,000)	17,000
Mkude`s current account will be credited with (£3,000+£500+ £ 8,000)	11,500
	———
Net profit shown in first part of profit and loss account	71,000

Limited company

When the net profit has been ascertained, the directors of company have to decide how much they can release as dividends and how much to retain. A limited company distributes its profits by means of dividends on the shares of its capital held by the shareholders. So, where a company declares a dividend of 10 per cent, the holder of each £1 share will receive dividends paid on other classes of shares.

Director`s fees should be debited to the profit and loss account proper. (if, however, these fees vary according to the amount of net profit paid and have to be passed by the company in general meeting, they should be kept in suspense until such meeting has taken place. Then they should be debited to the appropriation account. Because they are a proportion of profits due to the directors.)

When dividends and any other items have been debited to the appropriation account, the whole of the profit not have been used. The balance remaining is carried forward to the appropriation account of the next trading period.

When a company makes a large profit, the directors will deem it prudent to place a appropriation of such profit on one side, instead of distributing it amongst the shareholders. An account is opened to which such sums will be credited, the appropriation account being debited. This account is known as **reserve account** and contains appropriation from net profit, accumulating year by year.

Question for Practice

2. From the following balance appearing in the ledger of the New Manufacturing Co. On 31 December, draw up the profit and loss account for the year ended 31 December.

	£	£
Discounts allowed	32	
Discounts received		267
Gross profit brought down from trading		
Account		127,881
Salaries	44,261	
Bank charges	193	
Sundry office expenses	1,361	
Rent and rates	19,421	
Bad debts written off	937	
Carriage outwards	5,971	
Plant and machinery	50,000	

Notes:

(a) Write off per cent depreciation on plant and machinery.
(b) Rent owing on December amounted to £2,000.
(c) An insurance premium amounting to £500 was paid in July in the current year for the year to 30 June of the following year. The £500 is included in sundry office expenses.

Now check your answer with that provided at the end of the unit

E. THE NATURE OF A BALANCE SHEET

As we have seen, at the end of an accounting period, it is usual to extract a trial balance. From the trail balance are compiled the trading account, manufacturing account (if any), profit and loss appropriation account. In preparing these final accounts, many accounts in the ledger are closed, e.g. sales account is closed by being transferred to the credit of the trading account.

When the final accounts have been prepared, there will still be a number of larger accounts which remain open. These open account balances are extracted as a kind of final trial balance, set out in full detail and this final balance is known as the balance sheet.

A balance sheet is a statement showing the assets owned and the liabilities owed by the business on a certain dates. It can be ruled in account from, but it is not an account. However, the expression "final account" includes the balance sheet even though it is no really an account.

Because it is a statement as at a particular date, it is headed:

Name of firm
Balance Sheet as at (or as on at) date

It is **never** headed "for the year (other period) ended ……." This latter type of heading is used for trading and profit and loss account which cover a period of time.
The balance sheet may be presented with the assets on one side and the liabilities on the other. An alternative is to show the assets (net) first, with a total, and then the capital of the business, with its own total, in a vertical format. The vertical format is now the more generally used one.

Difference between Trial Balance Sheet and Balance Sheet

- A trial balance list of **all** the ledger balances, not only assets and liabilities but also gain and loss. A balance sheet is a list of a **part** only of the ledger balances, i.e. those remaining after the profit and loss items have been dealt with, the assets and liabilities.

- A trial balance is prepared **before** the revenue accounts are compiled. A balance sheet is prepared **after** the revenue account has been dealt with.

With the profit and loss account we actually transfer the gains and losses appearing in account in the books. Because the balance sheet is a statement and not an account, the accounts for assets and liabilities in the books are not affected when we draw up the balance sheet. We do not "transfer" them to the balance sheet.

Functions of the Balance Sheet

(a) Financial Position of Business

The balance sheet is drawn up in order to give a picture of the financial position of the business. It reveals whether the business is solvent. It shows how much is invested in different forms of property, and how the business is funded.

(b) Arithmetical Accuracy of Accounts

The agreement of the balance sheet also provides a check on the accuracy of the revenue account in much the same way as the agreement of a trial balance provides evidence of the arithmetical accuracy of the books.

(c) Bridge between Financial Years

The balance sheet is also a bridge between one financial year and the next. All accounts which remain open after the manufacturing, trading and profit and loss accounts have been prepared are summarized in the balance sheet.

Summarized Statement

If we listed each asset, each piece of machinery, each book debt etc. separately, the balance sheet would be extremely long. Assets and liabilities are summarized or grouped, therefore, into main classes, and only the total of each type is shown on the balance sheet. Thus, if our trade receivables are Jones, who owes us £10, and Smith, who owes us £15, we show under current assets:

Trade receivables £25

Summarization entails giving as much information in as little space as possible. Style and layout are important. As an example, assume that office furniture was worth £2,000 at the beginning of the year and has since depreciated by £100. The balance sheet will show:

Balance Sheet as at 31 December year 1

	£	£
Non-current assets		
Office furniture		
Balance 1 January	2,000	
less D*epreciation for year at 5%* par 100		1,900

F. ASSETS AND LIABILITIES IN THE BALANCE SHEET

Type of Asset

The key distribution to make is between fixed and current assets.

- **Non-Current Assets.**
  These are assets which are retained in a business, more or less permanently, for the purpose of earning revenue only and not for the purpose of sale.
  Examples are: plant, machinery, land, building, and vehicle. Some non-current assets are consumed by the passing of time, e.g. leases, mines. The difference between tangible and intangible assets is discussed later.

- **Current Assets**
  Cash and those other assets which have been made or purchased merely to be sold and converted into cash are known as current assets. It is form the turnover of current assets that a business makes its trading profit. Examples are: inventory in trade, trade receivables, cash, and temporary investments. Such assets are held for a short period only,e.g. inventory when sold creates trade receivables, these trade receivables circle moves round and current assets are kept constantly moving .

  Whether an asset is fixed or current depends entirely upon the kind of business. What is a fixed asset in one firm may be a current asset in another. For example, machinery is a fixed asset when held by a firm which manufactures cigarettes but, in the hands of a firm which who sells machinery, it will be a current asset. A motor van will be a fixed asset for a tradesman who uses it for delivery but, to a manufacturer of such vans, it will be a current asset, i.e. inventory.

  The deciding factor is whether the asset is held merely until purchaser can be found, or permanently for use in the business.
  However, you must member that even if an asset is not easily realizable, it may still be a current asset, e.g. a debt from a foreign importer may be hard to realize, owing to exchange restrictions, but it still remains a current asset. (Note also that a fixed asset is not necessarily immovable.)
  A further classification of assets may be made to distinguish between tangible and intangible assets.

- Assets which can be possessed in a physics sense, e.g. plant, machinery, land and buildings, are **tangible** assets. Also include in the category of tangible assets are legal right third parties.
- On the other hand, assets which cannot to possess in a physical sense, and which are not legal right against external persons, are intangible. Goodwill is perhaps the best example of an intangible asset. It is often very valuable asset in the case of an old-established business.

Valuation of Assets
Generally speaking, non-current assets represent money which has been spent in the past on items which were intended to be used to earn revenue for the firm. In many cases these non-current assets depreciate over a period of years and may finally have to be scrapped. Therefore, the money spent originally on a fixed asset should be spread out

over the number of years of the segmented life of the asset. An item representing depreciation will be debited to the profit and loss account annually.

Because we deduct the depreciation from the cost of the asset, the fixed asset is shown as a diminishing figure in the balance sheet each year (unless, of course, there have been addition to the asset during the year). The decrease in the value of the fixed asset is also shown as an expense in the annual profit and loss account.

Remember that not all no-current assets are consumed by the passing of time. Some, in fact, may appreciate, e.g. freehold land and buildings. With the rising value of such assets, it is considered quite correct to revalue them so the balance sheet shown the correct market value.

Current assets such as inventory are normally held for a relatively short period, i.e. until they can be realized. Current assets should generally be valued at cost or market price whichever is lower. This is necessary to ensure that no account is taken of profit until the assets have been realized.

Order of Assets in the Balance Sheet

The assets in the balance sheet must be arranged in a clear and logical order. The order usually adopted is:

    Non-current assets

    Current assets

In each group assets are arranged in an order from most fixed to most fluid, thus:

Non – current assets	Current Assets
Goodwill	Work in progress
Patents, trademarker,etc.	Inventory in trade
Freehold land and buildings	Trade receivables
Leasehold land and buildings	Payments in advance
Plant and machinery	Temporary investments
Motor vehicles	Bank deposit account
Furniture and fittings	Cash at bank
Long-time investment	Cash in hand

A sub-total for each group is extended into the end column of the balance sheet. The examples which follow later make this clear.

Liabilities to Proprietors

The liability of business to the proprietor is, in the case of sole, his capital account, i.e. the amount by which the business is indicated to him.

With a partnership, the liabilities to the proprietors are found in the capital accounts and current accounts of the partners. (The current accounts are only liabilities when they are credit accounts are only liabilities when they are credit balances. When they are debit balances they appear in the asset section of the balance sheet, since debit balances represented debts due from partners). The balances of these accounts represent in the indebtedness of the business to the various partners. With a limited company, this indebtedness is the amount of the share capital paid up.

The indebtedness of the business to the proprietor (s) cannot, strictly speaking, be classed as a liability. The proprietors of a firm can only with draw their capital in bulk when the firm is wound up, and even then they must wait until the outside trade payables have been satisfied. When the outside trade payaarables have been paid out of the proceeds of sale of the assets, it may be that there is very little left for the proprietors to take.

In some cases the proceeds of sale of the assets are insufficient to pay of the external trade payables. The proprietors must then provide more funds until the trade payarables are satisfied:

- A **sole trader** must contribute funds to pay off remaining outside trade payarables, even if this takes the whole of his private property and investments.
- In a **partnership**, the partners to must make good a deficiency on winding up. They must contribute until all the external trade payarables are paid, even if this takes the whole of their private means.
- A **limited liability company** is different from either a sole trader or a partnership, since the liability of each proprietor, i.e. shareholder, is restricted to the amount the originally agreed to contribute. For example, a shareholder has 100 shares of £1 each in a company, and has paid 75p on each share. He can only be called upon to pay a further sum of 25p per share (total £25), if the assets of the company do not realize sufficient to satisfy the external trade payables. In most companies all the shares are fully paid, so the shareholders are not liable for anything further.

External Liabilities
The external liabilities of any firm are those which cannot be described as indebtedness to proprietors. It is possible, however, for a person to be an external creditor and a proprietor. This occurs when a shareholder of a company becomes an ordinary trade creditor of the company in the normal course of business.

We can classify external liabilities in various ways:

(a)   **Long term or Current Liabilities**

- *Long-term Liabilities*

  Long-term liabilities are those which would not normally be repaid within 12 months.

- *Current Liabilities (Short-term Liabilities)*

  Current liabilities consist of current trading debts due for payment in the near future. It is essential that long-term and current liabilities are stated separately in the balance sheet, so that shareholders and third parties can judge whether the current assets are sufficient to meet the current liabilities and also provide sufficient working capital. Current liabilities also include accrued expenses.

(b)   **Secured and Unsecured Liabilities**

- *Secured Liabilities*

  Liabilities for which a change has been given over certain or all of the assets of the firm are said to be secured. In such cases the creditor, in default of payment, can exercise his rights against the assets charged, to obtain a remedy. (an asset is "charged" when the creditor gives a loan on condition that he acquires the ownership of the asset if the loan is not repaid by the agreed date. The asset is security for the loan.) This is similar to a mortgage on a private house.

A charge may be either **fixed** or **floating.** A fixed charge is one which relates only to one particular asset, such as a building. On the other hand, a floating charge can be exercised over the whole of the class mentioned in the charge, present or future. Debenture is often secured by a floating charge on the whole of the assets of the company.

The floating charge does not "crystallize" until the charge is enforced, i.e. the creditor goes to court to obtain payment of his debt. When this occurs, the firm which granted the charge may not deal in any way with any of the assets included in the charge.

A floating charge is convenient to both borrower and lender. The borrower is allowed to deal as he chooses, in the ordinary course of business, with the assets covered by the charge, without having to obtain the permission of the lender. Also the lender is satisfied because he knows that his loan is well secured. With a fixed charge, however, the borrower could not sell the asset charge without the permission of the lender.

- *Unsecured Liabilities*

  Such liabilities are not secured by a charge over any of the assets of a firm. In the event of a winding-up of a business, the secured trade payables are satisfied out of the proceeds of the asset (s) over which they have a charge. Any surplus, together with the proceeds of uncharged assets, are reserved to satisfy first the preferential liabilities (described below) and then the unsecured liabilities. When all these liabilities have been met, the final surplus, if any, is shared by the proprietors.

(c) **Preferential Liabilities**

On the bankruptcy of a sole trader or partnership, or on the winding-up of a company, certain liabilities enjoy preference over others. These debts are known as preferential liabilities. Examples are unpaid wages and taxation. Preferential liabilities do not concern us in the preparation of a balance sheet of a continuing business.

(d) **Contingent Liabilities**

Liabilities which might arise in the future but which are not represented in the books of the firm concerned at the date of drawing up the balance sheet are said to be contingent.

An example of contingent liabilities is where the firm concerned is the involved in a law action at the date of the balance sheet. If there is a possibility that damages and/or costs will be awarded against the firm, a note to this effect should be added as a footnote to the balance sheet.

G. **DISTINCTION BETWEEN CAPITAL AND REVENUE**

As we mentioned earlier in the course, revenue expenditure constitutes a charge against profits and must be debited to profit and loss account, whereas capital expenditure comprises all expenditure incurred in the purchase of non-current assets for the purpose of earning income, and is shown in a balance sheet. Failure to observe the distinction inevitably falsifies the results of the bookkeeping.

For example, if a motor car were purchased and the cost charged to profit and loss account as motor car expenses, or if a building were sold and the proceeds credited to profit and loss account as a trading gain, then both the profit and loss account and the balance sheet would be incorrect. It would not show a true fair view of the company's trading position.

Definitions

(a) **Capital Expenditure**

Where expenditure is incurred in acquiring, or increasing the value of, a permanent asset which is frequently or continuously used to earn revenue, it is capital expenditure.

(b)   Revenue Expenditure

This represents all other expenditure incurred running a business. Including expenditure necessary for maintaining the earning capacity of the business and for the upkeep of non-current assets in a fully efficient state.

It is extremely difficult to lay down a hard and fast rule as to the dividing line which separates capital expenditure and revenue expenditure. For example, if a general dealer bought a motor car, the cost would be debited to capital, whereas if a motor dealer bought the car, the cost would be debited to revenue and/or holding inventory, if not sold during the same accounting period as the purchase.

Capital and Revenue Receipts

The division of receipts into capital and revenue items is not nearly as difficult, as the source of receipts are generally far less in number than the types of expenditure.

(a)   Capital Receipt

These normally consist of additional payments of capital into the business, and proceeds from the sale of non-current assets.

(b)   Revenue Receipts

These comprise all other forms of income, including income form the sale of goods in the ordinary course of trading, interest on investments, rents, commission and discounts.

H.   PREPARATION OF FINANCIAL STATEMENT

Let's now see how Financial statements are prepared in practice for sole traders and partnerships company balance sheets follow the same lines, and we will look at these later.

Sole Trader

As an example, the financial statement of Mwanawetu is shown below.

Mwanawetu

Financial Statement as at 31 Dec............

81

	£	£	£
Non-current assets	Cost	Dep'n	Net
Freehold premises	21,480		21,480
Fixture and fittings	2,000	(100)	1,900
	23,480	(100)	
Current Assets			
Trading inventory	11,480		
Trade receivables	18,960		
less provision for bad debts	(750)		
	18,210		
Insurance prepaid	250		
Cash	240	30,180	
Current Liabilities			
Trade payables	19,490		
Accrued expenses	480	(19,790)	
Net current assets			10,210
Total assets less current liabilities			33,590
Long-term liabilities			
Mortgage on freehold			(12,470)
			21,120
Capital account			
Balance brought forward			18,000
Add Net profit for the year			14,010
			32,010
less Drawings			(10,890)
			21,120

Partnership

The main point of difference between the balance sheet of a sole trader and of a partnership lies in the capital and current account. While the sole trader may merge profits and losses, drawings, etc. into his capital account, this is not so in partnership. Current accounts are necessary to record shapes of profit and losses, interest on capitals, salaries, drawings, etc. and the final balance only need shown in the balance sheet.

The order of assets and liabilities is generally as shown in the balance sheet above for the sole trader. Current account always appears below capital accounts.

Here is a summarized version of the proprietors` interest section of the financial statement of a partnership:

Magoti, Ruta and Chemundungwao
Financial Statement as at 31 October…..

	Magoti £	Rutas £	Chemundugwao £	Total £
Proprietors` Interest				
Capital accounts	7,500	5,500	2,500	15,500
Current accounts	2,475	1,965	1,180	5,620
	9,975	7,465	3,680	21,120

Note that the formats we have used for the presentation of the accounts/financial statements in this unit are suitable for the type of business referred to, but when, in later study units, we deal with large companies who have to report under IGAAP, the format will be slightly different.

Questions for Practice

3. The following balances remain in Wiliam Dean`s books after he has completed his profit and loss account for the year ended 31 May Year 2:

	£	£
Capital 1 June Year 1		124,000
Net profit for year ended 31 May Year 2		13,570
Loan form John Dean (repayable in 10 years'		
time)		9,500
Trade payables		1,950
Premises	110,000	
Inventory	25,000	
Trade receivables	2,600	
Balance at bank	1,400	
Cash in hand	20	
Drawings (taken out of business for private use)	10,000	

Set out William Dean`s balance sheet as at 31 May Year 2.

Now check you answer with that provided at the end of the unit

ANSWERS TO QUESTIONS FOR PRACTICE

1. (a)

H. Smith & Co.
Trading Account year ended 31 October

	£	£	£
Sales		40,000	
less Returns		1,460	39,370
Cost of goods sold:			
Opening inventory		6,720	
Purchases	24,720		
Less Returns	(1,230)	23,490	
Carriage inwards		2,480	
		32,690	
Closing inventory		(7,630)	(25,060)
Gross profit			14,310

(b)   The profit would be increased by £500 to £14,810 because the net sales would be increased to £39,870 and the drawings account of Mr. Smith would be debited by similar amount, i.e. £500.

2.   **New Manufacturing Company**
                        Profit and loss Account for year ended 31 Dec

	£	£	£
Gross profit on trading		127,881	
Discount s received		267	128,148
Expenses			
Rent &rates (19,421+2,000)	21,421		
Salaries	44,261		
Sundries (1,361-250)	1,111		
Discounts allowed	32		
Bad debt	937		
Carriage outwards	5,971		
Bank charge	193		
Depreciation on plant and machinery:			
10% of £50,000	5.000		(78,926)
Net profit			49,222

Notes

- Rent and rates have been increased by £2,000, this being the amount owing at the year end.
- Sundry office expenses have been reduced by £250, this being the prepayment of the insurance premium.

3.

William Dean
Balance Sheet as at May year 2

	£	£
Non-current assets		
Premises		110,000
Current assets		
Inventory	25,000	
Trade receivables	2,600	
Balance at bank	1,400	
Cash in hand	20	
	29,020	
less **Current Liabilities**		
Trade payables	(1,950)	27,070
Net assets		137,070
Long-Term Liabilities		
Long-term loan (repayable in 10 years` time)		(9,500)
		127,570
Financed by:		
Opening capital		124,000
add Net profit		13,570
		137,570
less Drawings		127,570

INTRODUCTION

When a business draws up its own final accounts/financial statements for internal use, it may use any format it likes since there are no rules to prevent such accounts being drafted in the manner most suitable for management.

However, the published accounts of a business must be in accordance with the rules laid down in the legal framework of the country the business is resident in. they will also have to comply with relevant accounting standards (with which we will deal later). As a flavor of the legal regulations of country, we shall briefly deal with those of the UK in the following.

A. THE UK COMPANIES ACT 1985 AND ACCOUNTING REQUIREMENTS.

Background.

Even under the Companies Act 1929, the Act that operated before the Companies Act 1948 came into force, the directors of a company were under an obligation to lay before the members in general meeting, at least once every year, a balance sheet and a profit and loss account made up to the same date. However, with very few exceptions, that Act did not specify which deals were to be shown in this published profit and loss account. While the "internal accounts" (i.e. the final accounts drawn up for the information of the directors and management) would be fully detailed, the published profit and loss account frequently contained the barest minimum of information. Thus, it might show little else but that opening balance on the appropriation account, the "net profit" for the current year (a figure arrived at by deducing from true net profit all taxation, transfers to reserve, etc), and the balance on the appropriation account at the end of the year.

The following reasons led to the passing of the passing of the 1948 Act:

- The very real possibility that shareholders could be misled by published accounts.
- The growing need for more statistics relating to the commercial and business life of the country.
- It was thought to be in the public interest for the press to have as much information as possible about company finance.
- It was felt described to increase the amount of control which it was possible for shareholders to exercise over the running of the business.

Other Companies Acts were passed in 1967, 1976 and 1980, further increasing the amount of information required to be published by companies. The 1981 Act changed considerably the format of annual financial statements. The accounting provisions o these Acts were consolidated in the Companies Act 1985.

Before we consider the detailed provisions of the Companies Act 1985 regarding the content of published accounts, we must first study the requirements concerning their preparation, authorization and circulation to members.

Accounting Records and Reports

The provisions in respect of accounting records and reported are laid down in section 221 of the Companies Act 1985.

A Company must keep accounting that is sufficient to give a clear indication of its financial position at any time. The accounting records must be kept for three years in the case of a private Company, or six years otherwise and they must show:

- Daily records of receipts and payments of moneys
- Details of assets and liabilities
- Stocktaking records at the end of the financial year
- With the exception of retail sales, clear indications of identities of the purchasers and sellers of goods, as well as of the actual goods themselves.

From the above records, the following must be prepared at specific intervals:

- A profit and loss account (or an income and expenditure account, if appropriate)
- A balance sheet (as at the date of the end of the period covered by the profit and loss account)
- An auditors' report
- A directors' report
- Group account (if applicable).

Duty to Deliver Accounts

The provisions in respect of the duty to deliver accounts are laid down in section 227 of the Companies Act 1985.

Signing of Balance Sheet

The provisions in respect of the signing of the balance are laid down in section 238 of the Companies Act 1985.

The three provisions of which you must be aware are:

- Every balance sheet of a company must be signed on behalf of the board by two directors, or by the single director if there is only one. (Note that this is the company's own balance sheet and not, in case of a company with subsidiaries, the consolidated balance sheet)
- A balance sheet of a banking company must be signed by the secretary or manager and by at least three directors.
- If any copy of a balance sheet not so signed is issued, the company and every officer in default is liable to a fine not exceeding one-fifth of the statutory minimum (currently, the statutory minimum is £1,000).

Circulation of Published Accounts

The provisions in respect of the circulation of published accounts are laid down in section 240 of the Companies Act 1985.

- A copy of every balance sheet, profit and loss account, directors' report and auditors' report must be circulated to every shareholder and debenture holder at least 21 days before the meeting to discuss them.

- Any member or debenture holder is entitled to be supplied, within seven days of demand, with a copy of the last balance sheet, and documents required to be attached, free of charge.

Small and Medium – sized Companies – power to file Modified Statements

Section 248 of the Companies Act 1985 defines a company ads small or medium –sized if it satisfied two or more of the qualifying conditions below, in respect of any financial year of the company and the financial year immediately preceding that year. As at December 2007, these qualifying conditions are that:

- The amounts of its turnover not exceed £5.6m.
- Its balance sheet total must not exceed £2.8m. (Balance sheet total mans the total must assets before deduction of any liabilities).
- The average number of persons employed by the company in the financial year in question must not exceed 50.

Small and medium-sized companies are permitted to file modified financial statements (now termed "filling exemptions" as follows:

To be forwarded to registrar	Small Company	Medium Company
Balance sheet	Abridged	Full
Profit and loss account	None	Abridged
Directors' report	None	Full
Notes to accounts	Reduced	No need to disclose turnover or margin of gross profit
Information on director's and Employees' salaries	None	Full disclose

Note that these concessions relate only to documents filed with the Registrar. They do not affect the information that must be given to members of the company-and thus they actually involve more work for the company in preparing two sets of financial statements.

The filing exemption does not apply to a public company or a banking, insurance or shipping company, which must file full accounts irrespective of size.

If directors file such modified statements with the Registrar, they must include a special auditors' report which:

- States that the auditors consider that the requirements for exemption from filing full accounts are satisfied.

- Reproduces the full text of the auditors' report on the financial statements issued to members of the company.

Director's Report

A report by the directors must be attached to every balance sheet laid before a company in general meeting (S.235 Ca 1985). It must contain the following:

(a) A fair review of the development of the business of the company and its subsidiaries during the financial year ended with the balance sheet date, and of their position at the end of it.
(b) Details of the dividends proposed.
(c) A detail of transfers to resaves.
(d) Details of the principal activities of the company and subsidiaries, and any significant changes during the period.
(e) Any significant changes during the period in the fixed assets of the company or subsidiaries.
(f) Any significant differences between the market values and book values of land and buildings or any of the company's subsidiaries.
(g) The following details of the company or subsidiaries:
- Research and development activities.
- Likely future business developments.
- Any important events occurring since the final year-end
(h) Details of the interests in group shares or debentures they appear in the register of directors' interests at:
- The start of the period, or the date of the director's appointment, if later, and
- The end of the period.

This information must be given for each director at the end of the financial year, either here or in the notes to the accounts. A nil statement must be made, where applicable.

(i) Details of any political and charitable contributions over £300 in value in total.
(j) If the employees' average number is more than 250 during the financial year, details of the policy regarding:
- Employment of the disabled
- Continued employment and training of those who are disabled during employment in the country.
- Training, promotion and career development of the disabled.
(k) Full details of any disposals or purchase of a company's own shares.

Auditors' Report

The provisions in respect of an auditors' report are laid down in section 236 of the Companies Act 1985.

The auditors must make a report to the members on the accounts examined by them and on every balance sheet and profit and loss account laid before the company in general meeting. The report-which may be drawn up at some future time-must state:

(a) Whether, in their opinion, the company's balance sheet and profit and loss account have been properly prepared in accordance with the law.

(b) Whether, in their opinion, a true and fair view is given:
- In the case of the balance sheet, of the state of the company's affairs at the end of its financial year.
- In the case of the profit and loss account, of the company's profit or loss for its financial year.
- In the case of group accounts, of the state of affairs and profit or loss of the company and its subsidiaries, so far as concerns members of the company.

The Accounting standards Committee sought legal advice concerning the definition of "true and fair", and a summary of Counsel's opinion is as follows:

(i) "True and fair" evolves as times change.

(ii) The legal requirements, such as the formats contained in the Companies Act 1985, are guidelines offered by parliament at the time of drafting the legislation. It is conceivable that they could be superseded by accounting practice in order to give a true and fair view-e.g. if an SSAP were to say that historical cost accounting would been to give a true and fair view in time other alternative, then the courts might well accept the fundamentally altered true and fair view.

(iii) SSAPs are documents embodying seriously and deeply considered accounting matters that are accepted by the profession. Although the courts may disregard their terms, their requirements are likely to indicate a "true and fair" view of the handling of specific accounting problems, and they are likely to be used by the courts as influential guidelines. However, SSAPs evolve, and it must be accepted that what is "true and fair" when an SSAPs evolve, and it must be accepted that what is "true and fair" when an SSAPs is originally written may not be considered "true and fair" at some future date. Accurate and comprehensive disclosure of information within acceptable limits is important.

(iv) Overtime, the meaning of "true and fair" will remain the same but the content will differ.

It is the duty of the auditors to carry out such investigations as will enable them to form an opinion as to whether.

- Proper books of account have been kept by the company, and proper returns adequate for audit have been received from branches not visited by them.
- The company's final accounts are in agreement with these books and returns.

If their opinion is that proper books have not been kept, or adequate returns have not been received, or the final accounts do not agree with them, they must state this in their report.

The report of the auditors must be read before the company in general meeting.

You should note that auditors are also bound to consider-and report, if necessary-whether the accounts of the company comply with standard accounting practice. Normally an auditors' report is very short, stating that their, in their view, the accounts have been properly prepared, given a true and fair view of the profit or loss, etc. and comply with the companies Act and with standard accounting practice. The report can then be qualified by starting the respects in the accounts do not conform to the requirements.

B. THE BALANCE SHEET

Let us now return to the international requirements for the presentation of financial statements as contained in IASs.

Disclosure of Accounting Polices

Under IAS 1 presentation of financial statements, business must publish their financial statements every year. The information provided to shareholders (and other interested practices) would be of little value were there no explanation of the way in which the figures had been complied. IAS 1 addresses just this area-namely a business's accounting polices.

IAS 1 requires the production of a summary of significant accounting polices in which a business must disclosure the measurement basis used in preparing the financial statements and the other accounting polices that are relevant to an understanding of the financial statements. For example, users will need to be informed whether historical cost, current cost, net realizable value, fair value or recoverable amount has been expensed (see study unit 7) or capitalized as part a qualifying asset. Polices in respect of goodwill and foreign currency exchange will need disclosing as well as many others.

The statements of accounting plices from a business can run into several pages and we include an example from Tesco plc here for you to review-see Appendix 1. You may find other examples on the internet-try searching for the financial statements of an international business that you deal with regularly (such as Microsoft or McDonalds).

Presentation of the Balance Sheet

IAS 1 states that a balance sheet must be included in the financial statements, but does not give us a prescribed format in the actual standard (only in an appendix to it). It does, however, state the minimum information that must be presented on the face of the balance sheet in terms of line items for each of the following.

- Property, plant and equipment
- Investment property
- Intangible assets
- Investments accounted for using the equity method (see study unit 11 and 12)
- Biological assets
- Inventories
- Trade and other receivables
- Cash and cash equipments
- Trade and other payables
- Provisions
- Financial liabilities
- Deferred tax and assets
- Minority interests presented within equity (see study units 11 and 12)
- Issues capital and reserves.

As an illustration of this, we present below the balance sheet of Tesco plc for the year ended 24 February 2007.

Tesco PLC: Group Balance Sheet, as at 24 February 2007

	2007 £m	2006 £m
Non-current assets		
Goodwill and other intangible assets	2,045	1,525
Property, plant and equipment	16,976	15,882
Investment property	856	745
Investments in joint ventures and associates	314	476
Other investments	8	4
Deferred tax assets	32	12
	20,231	18,644
Current assets		
Inventories	1,931	1,464
Trade and other receivables	1,079	892
Derivative financial instruments	108	70
Current tax assets	8	-
Cash and cash equivalents	1,042	1,325
	4,168	3,751
Non-current assets classified as held for sale and assets of the Disposal group	408	168
	4,576	3,919
Current liabilities		
Trade and other payables	(6,046)	(5,083)
Financial liabilities:		

Borrowings	(1,554)	(1,646)
Derivative financial instruments and other liabilities	(87)	(239)
Current tax liabilities	(461)	(462)
Provisions	(4)	(2)
	(8,152)	(7,432)
Liabilities directly associated with the disposal group	-	(86)
	(8,152)	(7,518)
Net current liabilities	(3,576)	(3,599)
Non-current liabilities		
Financial liabilities		
Borrowings	(4,146)	(3,742)
Derivative financial instruments and other liabilities	(399)	(294)
Post-employment benefit obligations	(950)	(1,211)
Other non-current liabilities	(29)	(29)
Deferred tax liabilities	(535)	(320)
Provisions	(2)	(5)
	(6,084)	(5,601)
Net assets	10,571	9,444

Equity		
Share capital	397	395
Share premium account	4,376	3,988
Other reserves	40	40
Retained earnings	5,693	4,957
Equity attributable to equity holders of the parent	10,506	9,380
Minority interests	65	64
Total equity	10,571	9,444

As you can see from this example, non-current assets, current assets, current liabilities and non-current liabilities are all sub-totaled and added to give a total for net assets. This net assets figure is then represented by equity in the bottom half of the balance sheet.

In a simplified form this presentation is as follows:

NET ASSETS

Non-current assets;

 Intangible assets including goodwill and development
 Tangible assets:
 Property plant and equipment
Investment property
Deferred tax assets
Current assets

Inventories
Trade and other receivables
Cash and cash equivalents
Current liabilities
Trade and other payables
Provisions
Short-term loans and overdrafts
Net current assets (current assets less current liabilities)
Non-current liabilities
Loans
Deferred tax liabilities
Total of net assets
(Non-current assets, plus net current assets, less non-current liabilities)

EQUITY
Share capital
Share premium account
Revaluation reserves
Retained profits
Total of equity attributable to equity holders (the above items totaled)
Minority interests
Total equity
(Equity holders equity plus minority interests-this should equal net assets)

The format presentation in the appendix to IAS 1 actually shows both current liabilities and non-current liabilities in the bottom half of the balance sheet. The two halves of the balance sheet are retiled "assets" and "equity and liabilities". However, we find the presentation shown above gives better information to users and is the one commonly used by most international business. We suggest you use the style in your examinations, but as long as your balance sheet is in reasonable style you will not lose presentation marks.

Notes to the balance sheet are also required under IAS 1. In many cases, these can be very detailed and long, and we would refer you to the notes for Tesco on the Interest the cover almost 50 pages as an exemplar.

Example

The following example shows an acceptable layout of a balance sheet under IAS1.

J & K Plastics plc

Balance Sheet as at 31 December

	Current year £	Previous year £
Non-current Assets		
Intangible assets	X	X
Tangible assets	X	X
Investments	X	X
	X	X
Current Assets		
Inventories	X	X
Trade and other receivables	X	X
Cash at bank and in hand	X	X
	X	X
Current liabilities	(X)	(X)
Net current assets	X	X
Non-current liabilities	(X)	(X)
Provisions for liabilities and charges	(X)	(X)
	XXX	XXX
Capital and Reserves		
Called-up share capital	X	X
Share premium account	X	X
Revaluation reserves	X	X
Other reserves	X	X
Retained profits	X	X
	XXX	XXX

Approved by the Board (dates)   ……………..
Names of the (Directors)………………………

Note that previous year figures are also shown on the face of a balance sheet

An example of two important notes that are usually attached to all balance sheets follows.

Notes to the Financial Statement

(a) Intangible assets

	Development Costs	Patents & trademarks	Goodwill £	Total £
Cost				
At 1 Jan	X	X	X	X
Additions	X	X	X	X
Disposals	(X)	(X)	(X)	(X)
At 31 Dec	X	X	X	X
Amounts Written off				
Impairment				
At Jan 1 Balance	X	X	X	X
Charge for the year, IS etc	X	X	X	X
Deduction in respect of disposals	(X)	(X)	(X)	(X)
At 31 Dec	X	X	X	X
Net Book Values				
At 31 Dec current year	X	X	X	X
At 31 Dec previous year	X	X	X	X

(a) Tangibles assets

	Land & Buildings £	Plant & machinery £	Vehicles £	Total £
Cost or Valuation				
At 31 Jan	X	X	X	X
Additions	X	X	X	X
Revaluations (additional value only)	X	X	X	X
Disposals	(X)	(X)	(X)	(X)
At 31 Dec	X	X	X	X
Depreciation				
At Jan 1 balance	X	X	X	X
Charge for year IS	X	X	X	X
Deduction in respect of disposals	(X)	(X)	(X)	(X)
At 31 Dec	X	X	X	X
Net Book Value				

At 31 Dec current year	X	X	X	X
At 31 Dec previous year	X	X	X	X

THE INCOME STATEMENT

We will now consider the format of the income statement for publication..

Presentation of the Income Statement

IAS 1 requires an income statement to be prepared for each period as a minimum, the following items included:

- Revenue;
- Finance costs;
- Share of profit or loss associated and joint ventures;
- Tax expense;
- Profit or loss attributable to minority holders; and
- Profit or loss attributable to equity holders.

In the appendix IAS 1 we are presented with a typical income statement as follows:

1.	Revenue
2.	Cost of sales
3.	Gross profit or loss
4.	Other income
5.	Distribution expense
6.	Administrative expenses
7.	Other expenses
8.	Finance costs
9.	Share of profits of associates
10.	Profit before tax
11.	Income Tax expense
12.	Profit or loss for the financial year, attributable to:
	Equity holders of the parent
	Minority interest

Notes

- Revenue:- Should be shown and calculated net of trade discounts, VAT and other sales taxes.
- Notes must show the revenue broken down by classes of business and by geographical markets, having regard to the manner in which the company's activities addition information on revenue may be omitted if disclosure would be seriously prejudial to the company's interests.
- Cost of sales, distribution costs and administrative expenses have to be stipulated after taking any provision for depreciation or diminution of asset value into account. (Cost of sales is the direct expenses attributable to bringing the raw materials to the point of sale.)

- Dividend paid or payable to the shareholders is not shown on the face of the income statement. These are now required to be dealt with in new statement – "a statement of charges in equity" – as consider later in this study unit.

- Note also that extraordinary items do not exist any more according to the IASB. The IASB decided when revising IAS 8 in 2004 that, as extraordinary items (as they were previously called) resulted from the normal business risks faced by an entity, they do not warrant presentation in a separate part of the income and expense. A business can, if it wishes, disclose such items in the notes, but not on the face of the income statement.

- Finally, here you should note that earnings per share figures, both basic and diluted, are also disclosed on the face of the income statement, but they do not form part of the income statement. We will deal with EPS later in the course, in study unit 8.

We include here Wakulima's income statement as an exemple.

Wakulima : Group statement, year ended 24 February 2007

	2007 £m	2006 £m
Continuing operations		
Revenue (sales excluding VAT)	42,641	39,454
Cost of sales	(39,401)	(36,426)
Pensions adjustment-Finance Act 2006	258	-
Impairment of the Gerrads Cross site	(35)	-
Gross profit	3,463	3,028
Administrative expenses	(907)	(825)
Profit arising on property-related items	92	77
Operating profit	2,648	2,280
Share of post-tax profits of joint ventures and associates		
(Including £47m of property-related items (2005/06-£nil)	106	82
Profit on sale of investments in associates	25	-
Finance income	90	114
Finance costs	(216)	(241)
Profit before tax	2,653	2,235

Taxation	(772)	(649)
Profit for the year from continuing operations	1,881	1,586
Discontinued operation		
Profit/(loss)for the year from discontinued operation	18	(10)
Profit for the year	1,899	1,576
Attributable to:		
Equity holders of the parent	1,892	1,570
Minority interests	7	6
	1,899	1,576
Earnings per share from continuing and discontinued operations		
Basic	23.84p	20.07p
Diluted	23.54p	19.79p
Earning per share from continuing operations		
Basic	23.61p	20.20p
Diluted	23.31p	19.92p

- Note also that extraordinary items do not exist any more according to the AISB. The AISB decided when revising IAS 8 in 2004 that as extraordinary items (as they were previously called) resulted from the normal business risks face by an entity, they, do not warrant presentation in a separate part of the income statement. Thus, these items are now just a subset of items of income and expense. A business can, if it wishes, disclose such items in the notes, but on the face on the income statement.
- Finally, here, you should note that earnings per share figures, both basic and diluted, are disclosed on the face of the income statement, but they do not form part of the income statement. We will deal with EPS later in the course, in study unit 8.

We include here Wakulima`s income statement as an example.

Wakulima : group Income Statement year ended 24 February 2007

	2007 £m	2006 £m
Continuing operations		
Revenue (sales excluding VAT)	24,641	39,454
Cost of sales	(39,401)	(36,426)
Pensions adjustment – finance Act 2006	258	-
Impairment of the Garrard cross site	(35)	-
Gross profit	3,463	3,028
Administrative expenses	(907)	(825)
Profit arising on property-related items	92	77
Operating profit	2,648	2,280
Share of post-tax profits of joint ventures and associates		

(including £47m of property- related items (2005/06 -£nil)	106	82
Profit on sales of investments in associates	25	-
Finance income	90	114
Finance costs	(216)	(241)
Profit before tax	2,653	2,235
Taxation	(772)	(649)
Profit for the year from continuing operations	1,881	1,586
Discontinued operation		
Profit/(loss)for the year from discontinued operation	18	(10)
Profit for the year	1,899	1,576
Attributable to:		
Equity holders of the parent	1,892	1,570
Minority interests	7	6
	1,899	1,576

Earnings for share from continuing and discontinued operations		
Basic	23.84p	20.07p
Diluted	23.54p	19.79p
Earnings per share form continuing operations		
Basic	23.61p	20.20p
Diluted	23.31p	19.92p

Example of Internal and Published Income Statement

In order to see how one kind of income statement can be changed into another, study the example set out over the following pages.

(a) **Income Statement for Internal Distribution**

Mwanawapakaya (pty) Co Ltd
Income Statement for the Year ended 31 December

	£	£	£
Net sales			1,750,000
Less Cost of sales:			
Inventory 1 Jan	300,000		
Purchases	1,500,000		
	1,800,000		
Inventory 31 Dec	(400,000)		(1,400,000)
Gross profit			350,000
Distribution costs:			
Salaries & wages	40,000		
Motor vehicle costs	25,000		

General	20,000		
Depreciation: MV	7,000		
Depreciation: Machinery	3,000	95,000	
Administration expenses:			
Salaries & wages	45,000		
Director's remuneration	22,000		
Motor vehicle	12,000		
General	27,000		
Auditors	4,000		
Depreciation: Office furniture	3,000		
Depreciation: Office machinery	2,000	115,000	(210,000)
			140,000
Other operating income:			
Rents receivable			9,000
			149,000
Income from shares in associated companies		3,000	
Income from shares in non-related companies		1,500	
Other interest receivable		1,000	5,500
			154,500
Interest payable:			
Loans repayable in less than 5 years		5,500	
Loans repayable in less than 10 years		5,000	(10,500)
Profit on ordinary activities before taxation			144,000
Tax on profit on ordinary activities			(48,000)
Profit on ordinary tax			96,000
Undistributed profit brought forward from last year			45,000
			141,000
Transfer to general reserve		47,000	
Proposed ordinary dividend		60,000	(107,000)
Undistributed profits carried forward to next year			34,000

An appropriate from of published statement is shown below.

(b) **Income Statement for Publication**

Mwanawapakaya (pty) Ltd

Income Statement for the Year ended 31 December

	£	£
Revenue		1,750,000
Cost of sales		(1,400,000)
Gross profit		350,000
Distribution costs	95,000	
Administration costs	115,000	(210,000)
		140,000
Other income		11,500
Income from associated interests		3,000
		154,500
Finance costs		(10,500)
Profit before taxation		144,000
Tax expense		(48,000)
Profit for the year after taxation		96,000
Profit attributable to equity holders		96,000

C. IAS: STATEMENT OF CHARGES IN EQUITY

This is another primary statement required by IAS 1 as part of a complete set of published statements. This statement has now, as at October 2007, been split into two statements and we will deal with part separately.

Separate Statement of Comprehensive Income

This statement encompasses all those other items of income and expense that have not been include in the income statement, including such items as revaluation of non-current assets and foreign currency exchange differences. Profit for the year is also included.

We present below Serengeti's statement of comprehensive income – just note that they have titled it "statement of recognised income and expense" as it was produced before the charge in IAS 1.

Serengeti co.: group Statement of Recognized Income and Expense,

year ended 24 February 2007

	2007 £m	2006 £m
(Loss)/gain on revaluation of available-for-sale investments	(1)	2
Foreign currency translation differences	(65)	3
Total gain/(loss) on defined benefit pension schemes	114	(443)
(Losses)/gains on cash flow hedges:		
-Net fair value (losses)/gains	(26)	44
-Reclassified and reported in the Income Statement	(12)	(5)
Tax on items taken directly to equity in	12	133
Net Income/(expense) recognized directly in equity	22	(236)
Profit for the year	1,899	1,576
Total recognized income and expense for the year	1,921	1,340

Statement of Changes in Equity

This statement includes dividends and issues or redemptions shares. A typical statement would be as follows:

	Share capital	Other reserves	Translation reserve (foreign currencies)	Returned earnings	Total	Minority interest	Equity holders
Balance 20-1	X	X	(X)	X	X	X	X
Comprehensive income (from above statement which will include profit for the period)		X	(X)	X	X	X	X
Dividends				(X)	(X)	(X)	(X)
Issue of share capital	X				X		
Balance 20-2	X	X	(X)	X	X	X	X

D. SUMMARY OF STATEMENTS REQURED BY IAS 1

To summarize, a complete set of financial statements published in accordance with IAS 1comprises:

(a) A financialtatement
(b) An income statement
(c) A statement of comprehensive income
(d) A statement of charge in equity
(e) A cash flow statement (see study unit 5)
(f) Notes comprising a summary of significant accounting policies and other explanatory notes

All of these statements need to present fairly the financial position, financial performance and cash flows an entity. Fair presentation requires the faithful representation of the effect of transactions, other event and conditions in according in accordance with the definitions and recognition criteria for assets, liabilities, income, expense and equity. These are as follows:

- **Assets:** are resources controlled by the entity as a result of past events and from which future economic benefits are expected to flow to the entity.
- **Liabilities:** are present obligations of the entity arising from past events, the settlement of which is expected to result in an outflow from the entity of resource embodying economic benefits.
- **Income:** is the increase in economic benefits during the accounting period in the form of inflows or enhancements of assets or decreases of liabilities that result in increases in equity, other than those relating to contributions from equity participants.
- **Expenses:** are decreases in economic benefits during the accounting period in the form of outflows or depletions of assets or incurrence of liabilities that result in decreases in the equity, other than those relating to distributions to equity participants.
- **Equity:** is the residual interest in the assets of the entity after deducting all its liabilities.

E. NARRATIVE STATEMENTS REQUIRED IN PUBLISHED FINANCIAL STATEMENTS.

Annual reports of business also include several narrative reports. Many of these are required by the legislation of a particular country or by stock exchange requirements. We are not going to deal with the plethora of legislation in this area, but we will consider the following narrative reports;

- Audit report (see also study unit 1)
- Director`s reports
- Corporate governance report.

The audit Report

The auditor's report is made to shareholders and should give a clear opinion on the financial statements. It should also give the reasoning behind that opinion and state how the audit was carried out.

We include in Appendix 2 an example of an unqualified audit report from Tesco's annual report.

When auditors find problems during their audit they do not have the power to insist that financial statements are amended, although many business will amend them to take account of the auditor's findings. What they do have the power to do is to issue a modified or qualified audit report. This modified audit report alerts the shareholders to what they have discovered and expresses the auditor's opinion on whether this affects the truth and fairness of the financial statements audit generally consider the issue of a modified report as a last resort.

The Director's Report

This report is generally included in the annual report of a business. Within the United Kingdom, the Companies Act 1985 regulates it.

The report is done / designed to provide information that, might be omitted from the annual report. We include here, in Appendix 3, an example of directors' report taken from a company's annual report.

Corporate Governance Report

Corporate governance is defined by the organization for Economic Co-operation and Development (OECD) as:

"The system by which business corporations are directed and controlled. The corporate governance structure specifies the distribution of rights and responsibilities among different participants in the corporation, such as the board, managers, shareholders and other stakeholders, and spells out the rules and procedures for making decisions on corporate affairs. By doing this, it also provided the structure through which the business objectives are set, and the means of attaining those objectives and monitoring performance."

From the above definition we can see that corporate governance is multi-faceted it covers processes, systems and cultures amongst others, and from the view point of many stakeholders. Corporate governance has come to the fore since the collapse of such companies as Enron and World com.

In 2004, the OECD issued its updated principles of Corporate Governance and several countries issue its updated principles of Corporate Governance and several countries issue their own regulations-fir example, as a result of several reports, in the UK there is now a combined code on Corporate Governance issued by the Financial Reporting Council (in June 2006).

The OECD sees corporate governance as a key element in improving economic efficiency and growth as well as enhancing investor confidence. Good corporate governance should ensure that the directors and managers purpose objectives within the business that are in the interests of the business and its stakeholders, not just themselves. The aim of the report is to allow the reader to make a judgment on whether the corporate governance of the business is adequate to achieve this aim. Weak and non-transparent regimes can lead to unethical behavior in a business and ultimately loss of market integrity.

A Corporate Report will cover such matters as:

- Board composition and independence
- Board responsibilities
- Board processes and delegation regulations
- Appointments to the Board
- Determination of executive remuneration
- Audit committee
- Board performance evaluation.
- Risk management and internal controls
- Relations with stakeholders
- Compliance with any codes

The Corporate report run to 5 pages so we do not produce it here, but we do advise you to go to the internet and read it or indeed any other corporate report of a large multinational business.

Other Statements

The subject of reporting to stakeholders and the content of annual reports is on going and within annual reports you may see examples of the following:

- Social and environmental reports
- Past trends in key financial figures
- Value added statements
- Employment reports
- Statement of future prospects
- Management commentaries
- Operating and financial review

As we have stated previously you will enhance your understanding of this study unit if you access several annual reports that are freely available on the internet.

APPENDIX 1: EXAMPLE OF STATEMENT OF ACCOUNTING POLICES
(Z CO. LTD.)

The following extract is from Z Co.Ltd's Annual Report and Financial Statements, 2007-Note 1 to the Group Financial Statements (pages 48-55).

General information

Z Co. Ltd's is a public limited company incorporated in the United Kingdom under the Companies Act 1985 (Registration number 445790). The address of the registered office is Tesco House, Delamare Road, Cheshunt Hertfordshire, EN8 9SL, UK.

As described in the Director's Report, the main activity of the Group is that of retailing and associated activities.

Statement of compliance

The consolidated financial statements have been prepared in accordance with International Financial Reporting Standards (IFRS) and International Financial Reporting Interpretation Committee (IFRIC) interpretations as endorsed by the European Union, and those parts of the Companies Act 1985 applicable under IFRS.

Basis of preparation

The financial statements are presented in Pounds Sterling, rounded to the nearest million. They are prepared on the historical cost basis modified for the revaluation of certain financial instruments.

The according policies set out below have been applied consistently to all periods presented in these consolidated financial statements.

Basis of consolidation

The Group financial statements consist of the financial statement of the ultimate Parent Company (Z Co.Ltd) all entities controlled by the Company (its subsidiaries) and the Group's share of its interests in joint ventures and associates

Where necessary, adjustments are made to the financial statements of subsidiaries, joint ventures and associates to brig the accounting policies used into line with those of the Group.

Subsidiaries

A subsidiary is an entity whose operating and financing policies are controlled, directly or indirectly, by Z Co.Ltd.

The accounts of the Parent Company's subsidiary undertakings are prepared to dates around the Group year end apart from Hymall, which for this reporting period have been prepared to 31 December 2006. Hymall has a different year end to the Group, as it is yet to be aligned with the Group year end following its acquisition in December 2006.

The financial statements of subsidies are including in the consolidated financial statements from the date that control commences until the date that control ceases.

Intergroup balances and any unrealized gain and losses or income and expenses arising from intergroup transactions, are eliminated in preparing in the consolidated financial statements.

Joint ventures and associates

A joint venture is an entity in which the Group holds an interest on a long-term basis and which is jointly controlled by the Group and one or more other ventures under a contractual agreement.

An associate is an undertaking, not being a subsidiary or joint venture, over which the Group has significance and can participate in the financial and operating policy decisions of the entity.

The Group's share of the results of joint ventures and associates is include in the Group Income Statement using the equity method of accounting. Investment in joint ventures and associates are called in the Group Balance Sheet at cost plus post-acquisition changes in the Group's share of the net assets of the entity, lees any impairment in value. The carrying values of investments in joint ventures and associates include acquired goodwill.

If the Group's share of losses in a joint venture or associate equals or exceed its investment in the joint venture or associate, the Group does not recognize further losses, unless it has incurred obligations to do so or made payments on behalf of the joint venture or associate.

Unrealized gain arising from transactions with joint ventures and associates are eliminated to the extent of the Group's interest in the entity.

Use of assumptions and estimates

The preparation of the consolidated financial statements requires management to make judgments, estimates and assumptions that affect the application of policies and reported amounts of assets and liabilities, income and expenses. The testament and associated assumptions are based on historical experience and various other factors that are believe to be reasonable under the circumstances, the results of which from the basis of making judgments about carrying values of assets and liabilities that are not readily apparent from other sources. Actual results may differ from these estimates.

The estimates and underlying assumptions are reviewed on an ongoing basis. Revision to accounting estimates are recognized in the period in which the estimate is revised if the revision affect only that period, or in the period of the revision and future periods if the revision affects both current and future periods.

Critical estimates and assumptions are made in particular with regard to establishing uniform depreciation and amortization periods for the Group, impairment testing, assumptions for measuring pension provisions, determination of the fair value of obligation to purchase minority interests, classification of leases as operating leases versus finance leases (including on sale and leasebacks), the like hood that assets can be realized and the classification of certain operations as held for sale.

Revenue

Revenue consists of sales through retail outlets.

Revenue is recorded net of returns, relevant vouchers/offers and value-added taxes, when the significant risks and rewards of ownership have been transferred to the buyer. Relevant vouchers/offers include: money off coupons, conditional spend vouchers and offer such as buy one get one free (BOGOF) and 3 for 2. Commission income is recorded based on the term of the contracts.

Club card and loyalty initiatives

The cost of clubcard is treated as cost of sale, with an accrual equal to the estimated fair value of the points issued recognized when the original transaction occurs. On redemption, the cost of redemption is offset against the accrual.

The fair value of the points awarded is determined with reference to the cost of redemption and considers factors such as redemption via Club card deals versus money-off in store and redemption rate.

Computers for Schools and Sport for Schools and Clubs vouchers are issued by Tesco for redemption by participating schools/clubs and are part of our overall Community Plan. The cost of the redemption (i.e. meeting the obligation attached to the vouchers) is treated as a cost rather than as a deduction from sales.

Other income

Finance income is recognized in the period to which it relates on an accruals basis. Dividends are recognized when a legal entitlement to payment arises.

Operating profit

Operating profit is stated after profit arising on property – related item but before the share of results of joint ventures and associates, finance income and finance costs.

Discontinued operations

A discontinued operation is a component of the Group's business that represents a separate line of business or geographical area of operation occurs. Upon disposal or earlier, if the operation meets the criteria to be classified as held for sale, under IFRS 5 Non-current assets held for sale.

Property, plant and equivalent

Property, plant and equivalent assets are carried at cost less accumulated depreciation and any recognized impairment in value. Property, plant and equivalent assets are depreciated on a straight-line basis to their residual value over their anticipated useful economic lives

The following depreciation rates are applied for the Group:

- Freehold and leasehold buildings with greater than 40 years unexpired-at 2.5%of cost.
- Leasehold properties with less than 40 years unexpired are depreciated by annual installments over the unexpired period of the lease.
- Plant, equivalent, fixtures and fittings and motor vehicles-at rates varying from 9% to 33%.

Assets held under finance leases are depreciated over their expected useful lives on the same basis as owned assets or, when shorter, over term of the relevant lease.

All tangible fixied assets are reviewed for impermanent in accordance with IAS 36 'Impairment of Assets' when there are indications that the carrying value may not be recoverable.

Borrowing costs

Borrowing costs directly attributable to the acquisitions or construction of qualifying assets are capitalized. Qualifying assets are those that necessarily take a substantial period of time to prepare for their intended use. All other borrowing costs are recognized in the income statement in the period in the period in which they occur.

Investment property

Investment property is property held to earn rental income and/or for capital appreciation rather than for the purpose of Group operating activities. Investment property assets are carried at cost less accumulated depreciation and any recognized impairment in value. The depreciation policies for investment property are consistent with those described for owner-occupied property.

Leasing

Leases are classified as finance leases whenever the terms of the lease transfer substantially all the risk and rewards of ownership to the lease. All other leases are classified as operating leases.

The Group as a lesser

Amounts due from lasses under finance leases are recorded as perceivable at the amount of the groups net investment in the leases. Finance lease income is allocated to the accounting periods so as to reflect a constant periodic rate of return on the Groups net investment in the lease.

Rental income from operating leases is recognized on a straight-line basis over the term of the relevant lease.

The Group as a lease

Assets held under finance leases are recognized as assets of the Group at their fair value or, if lower, at the present value of the minimum lease payments, each determined at the inception of the lease. The corresponding liabilities are included in the Balance sheet as a finance lease obligation. Lease payments are apportioned between finance charges and reduction of the leas obligations so as to achieve a constant rate of interest on the remaining balance of the liability. Finance changes are charged to the income statement.

Rentals payable under operating leases are charged to the income statement on a straight-line basis over the term of the relevant lease.

Sales and leaseback

A sale and leaseback transaction is one where a vendor sells an asset and immediately requires the use of that assets by entering into a lease with the buyer. The accounting treatment of the sale an leaseback depends upon the substance of the transaction (by applying the lease classification principles described above) and whether or not the sale was made at the assets fair value.

For sale and finance leasebacks, any apparent profit or loss from the sale is deferred and amortized over the lease term. For sale and operating leasebacks, generally the assets are sold at fair value, and accordingly the profit or loss from the sale is recognized immediately.

Following initial recognition, the lease treatment is consistent with those principles described above.

Business combinations and goodwill

All business combinations are accounted for by applying the purchase method.

On acquisition, the assets and liabilities and contingent liabilities of an acquired entity are measured at their fair value. The interest of monitory shareholders is stated at the minority's proportion of the fair values of the assets and liabilities recognized.

Goodwill arising on consolidation represents the excess of the cost of an acquisition over the fair value of the Group's share of the net assets of the acquired subsidiary, joint venture or associate at the date of acquisition. If the cost of acquisition is less the than the fair value of the Group's share of the net assets of the acquired entity (i.e. a discount on an acquisition) then the difference is credited to the income statement in the period of acquisition.

At the acquisition date of a subsidiary, goodwill acquired is recognized as an asset and is allocated to each of the cash generating units expected to benefit from the business combination's synergies and to the lowest level at which management monitors the goodwill arising on the acquisition of joint ventures and associates is included within the carrying value of the investment.

Goodwill is received for impairment at least annually by assessing the recoverable amount of each cash-generating unit to which the goodwill relates. When the recoverable amount of the cash-generating unit is less than the carrying amount, an impairment loss is recognized.

Any impairment is recognized immediately in the income statement and is not subsequently reversed.

On disposal of a subsidiary, joint venture or associate, the attributable amount of goodwill is included in the determination of the profit or loss on disposal.

Goodwill arising on acquisitions before 29 February 2004 (the date of transition to IFRS) was retained at the previous UK GAAP amounts subject to being tested for impairments at that date. Goodwill written off to reserves under UK GAAP prior to 1998 has not been restated and will not be included in determining any subsequent profit or los on disposal.

Intangible assets

Acquired intangible assets

Acquired intangible assets, such as software or pharmacy licenses, are measured initially at cost and are amortized on a straight-line basis over their estimated useful lives.

Internally-generated intangible assets- Research and development expenditure. Research costs are expensed as incurred.

Development expenditure incurred on an individual project is carried forward only if all the criteria set out in IAS 38 'Intangible Assets' are met, namely:

- An asset is created that can be identified (such as software or new processes);
- It is probable that the asset created will generate future economic benefits; and
- The development cost of the asset can be measured reliably.

Following the initial recognition of development expenditure, the cost is amortized over the project's estimated useful; life, usefully at 4%-25%of cost per annum.

Impairment of tangible and intangible assets excluding goodwill.

At each Balance sheet date, the Group reviews the carrying amounts of its tangible and intangible assets to determine whether there is any indication that those assets have suffered an impairment loss. If such indication exists, the recoverable amount of the asset is estimated in order to determine the extent of the impairment loss (if any). Where the asset does not generate can flows that are independent from other assets, the Group estimates the removable amount of the cash-generating unit to which the asset belongs.

The recoverable amount is the higher of fair value less costs to sell, and value in use. In assessing value in use, the estimated future cash flows are discounted to their present value using a pre-tax discount rate of that reflects current market assessments of the time value of money and the risk specific to the asset.

If the recoverable amount of an asset(or cash-generating unit) amount of the asset (or cash-generating unit) is reduced to its recoverable amount. An impairment loss is recognized as an expense immediately.

Where in impairment loss subsequently reverses, the carrying amount of the asset (or cash-generating unit) is increased to the revised estimate of the recoverable amount, but so that the increased carrying amount does not exceed the carrying amount that would have been determined if no impairment loss had been recognized for the asset (or cash-generating unit) in prior years. A reversal of an impairment loss is recognized as income immediately.

Inventories

Inventories comprise goods held for resale and properties held for, or in the course of development and are valued at the lower of cost and fair value less costs to sell using the weighted average cost basis.

Cash and cash equivalents

Cash and cash equivalents in the Balance sheet consist of cash at bank and in hand short-term deposited with an original maturity of three months or less.

Non-current assets held for sale

Non-current assets and disposal groups are classified as held for sale if their carrying amount will be recovered through sale rather than continuing use. This condition is regarded as met only when the sale is highly probable and the asset (or disposal group) is available for immediate sale in its present condition. Management must be committed to the sale and it should be expected to be completed within one year from the date of classification.

Non-current (and disposal groups) classified held for sale are measured at the lower of carrying amount and fair value less costs to sell.

Pensions and similar obligation

The Group accounts for pensions and other post-employment benefits (principally private heath care) under IAS 19 Employee Benefits'.

In respect of defined benefit plans, obligations are measured at discounted present value (using the projected unit credit method) whit list plan assets are recorded at fair value. The operating and financing costs of such plans are recognized separately in the income statement; service costs are special systematically over the expected service lives of employees and financing costs are recognized in the periods in which they arise. Actuarial gains and loses are recognized immediately in the statement of Recognized income and Expense.

Payments to defined contribution schemes are recognized as an expense as they fall due.

Share-based payments.

Employees of the group receive part of their remuneration in the form of share-based payment transactions, where by employees render services in exchange for shares or rights over shares (equity-settled transactions).

The fair value of employee share option plans is calculated at the grant date using the Black-scholes model. In accordance with IFRS 2 'share based payment' the resulting cost is charged to the income statement over the vesting period. The value of the charge is adjusted to reflect expected and actual levels of vesting.

Taxation

The tax expense included in the income statement consists of current and differed tax.

Current tax is the expected tax payable on the taxable income for the year, using tax rates enacted or substantively enacted by the balance sheet date.

Tax is recognized in the income statement except to the extent that it relates to items recognized directly in equity, in which case it is recognized in equity.

Differed tax is provided using the balance sheet liability method, providing for temporary differences between the carrying amounts of assets and liabilities for financial reporting purposes and the amount used for taxation purposes.

Deferred tax is calculated at the tax rate s that have been enacted or substantively enacted by the balance sheet date. Deferred tax is charged or credited in the income statement, except when it relates to items charged or credited directly to equity, in which case the deferred tax is also recognized in equity.

Deferred tax assets are recognized to the extent that it is probable that taxable profits will be available against which deductible temporary differences can be utilized.

The carrying amount of deferred tax assets is reviewed at each balance sheet date and reduced to the extent that is no longer probable that sufficient taxable profits will be available to allow all or part of the asset to be recovered.

Deferred tax assets and liabilities are offset against each once when there is a legally enforceable right to set off current taxation assets against current taxation liabilities and it's the intention to settle these net bases

Foreign currents

Transactions is foreign currencies are transited at the exchange are on the date of the transaction. At each balance sheet date, monetary assets and liabilities that are denominated in foreign currencies are retranslated at the rates prevailing on the balance sheet date. All differences are taken to the income statement for the period.

The financial statements of foreign subsidiaries are translated into pounds steering according to the functional currency concept of IAS 21. The effects of changes in foreign exchange rates; since the majority of consolidated companies operate as independent entities within their local economic environment, their respective local currency is the functional currency. Therefore assets and liabilities of overseas subsidiaries denominated in foreign currencies are translated at exchange rates prevailing at the date of the group balance sheet, profits and loses are translated into pounds sterling at average exchange rate for the relevant accounting periods, exchange differences arising, if any are classified as equity and transferred to the groups

translation differences are recognized as income or expenses in the period in which the operation is disposed of.

Goodwill and fair value adjustments arising on the acquision of a foreign entity are treated as assets and liabilities of the foreign entity and translated at the closing rate.

Financial instruments

Financial assets and financial liabilities are recognized or the group's balance sheet when the group becomes a party to the contractual provision of the instrument.

Trade receivables

Trade receivables are non interest bearing and are recognized initially at fair value, and subsequently at amortized cost using the effective interest rate method reduced by appropriate allowances for estimated recoverable amounts.

Investments

Investments are recognized at trade date. Investments are classified as ether held for trading or available for sale and are recognized at fair value.

For held for trading investments, gains and losses arising from changes in fair value are recognized in the income statement.

For available for sale investments, gains and losses arising from changes in fair value are recognized directly in equity until the security is disposed of or is determined to be impaired at which time the cumuletetive gain or loss previously recognized in equity is included the net result for the period interest calculated using the effective interest rate method is recognized in the income statement. Dividends on an available-for sale equity instrument are recognized in the income statement when the entity's right to receive payment is established.

Financial liabilities

Financial liabilities and equity instruments are classified according to the substance of the nonfactual arrangements entered into. An equity instrument is any contract that gives a residual interest in the assets of the group after deducting all of its liabilities.

Interest-bearing borrowings

Interest bearing bank loans and overdrafts are initially recorded at fair value, net of attributable transaction costs. Subsequent to initial recognition, interest-bearing borrowing are stated at mortised cost with any difference between cost and redemption value being recognized in the income statement over the period of the borrowing on an effective interest basis.

Trade payable

Trade payable is non interest-bearing and is stated at mortised cost.

Equity instruments.

Equity instruments issued by the Company are recorded at the proceeds received, net of direct issue costs.

Derivative financial instruments and hedge accounting

The group uses derivative financial instruments to hedge it exposure to foreign exchange and interest rate risks arising from operating, financing and investment activities. The group does not hold or issue derivatives do not quality trading purposes however if derivatives do not quality for hedge accounting they are accounted for as such.

Derivative financial instruments are recognized and stated at fair value. The fair value of derivative financial instruments is determined by reference to market values for similar financial instruments, by discounted cash flows, or by the use of option valuation models. Where derivatives do not quality for hedge accounting, any gains or losses on remeasuremnt are immediately recognized in the income statement. Where derivatives qualify for hedge accounting, recognition of any resultant gain or loss depends on the nature of the hedge relationship and the being hedged.

In order to qualify for hedge accounting, the group is required to document from inception the relationship between the item being hedge and the hedging instrument. The group is also required to document and demonstrate an assessment of the relationship between the hedged item and the heading instrument which shows that the hedge will be highly effective on an ongoing basis. This effectiveness testing is performed at each period to ensure that the hedge remains highly effective.

Financial instruments with maturity dates of more than one year from the balance sheet date are disclosed as non-current.

Fair value hedging

Derivative financial instruments are classified as fair value hedges when they hedge the group's exposure to changes in the fair value of a recognized asset or liability. Changes in the fair value of derivatives that are designated and qualify as fair value hedges are recorded in the income statement together with any changes in the fair value of the hedged item that is attributable to the hedged risk.

Derivative financial instruments qualifying for fair value hedge accounting are principally interest rate swaps (including cross currency swaps).

Cash flow hedging

Derivative financing instruments are classified as cash flow hedges when they hedge the group's exposure to variability in cash flows that are either attributable to a particular risk associated with a recognized asset or liability or a highly probable forecasted transaction.

The effective element of any gain or loss from remeasuring the derivative instrument is recognized directly in equity.

The associated cumulative gain or loss is removed from equity and recognized in the income statement in the same period or periods during which the hedged transaction affects the income statement. The classification of the effective portion when recognized in the income statement is the

Net investment hedging

Derivative financial instruments are classified as net investment hedges when they hedge the group's net investment in an overseas operation. The effective element of any foreign exchange gain or loss from remeasuring the derivative is recognized directly in equity. Any ineffective element is recognized immediately in the income statement. Gains and losses accumulated in equity are included in the income statement when the foreign operation is disposed of.

Derivative instruments qualifying for net investment hedging are principally forward foreign exchange transactions and currency options.

Treatment of agreements to acquire minority interests

same as the classification of the derivative instrument which does not meet the criteria for an effective hedge is recognized immediately in the income statement within finance costs.

Derivative instruments qualifying for cash flow hedging are principally forward foreign exchange transactions and currency options.

Hedge accounting is discontinued when the hedging instrument expires is sold terminated or exercised, or no longer qualifies for hedge accounting. At that point in time, any cumulative gain or loss on the hedging instrument recognized in equity is retailed in equity until the forecasted transaction occurs. If a hedged transaction is no longer expected to occur, the net cumulative gain or loss recognized in equity is transferred to the income statement.

The group has entered into a number of agreements to purchase the remaining shares of subsidiaries with minority shareholdings.

Under IAS 32 'Financial instruments: Disclosure ' the net present value of the expected future payments are shown as a financial liability. At the end of each period, the valuation of the liability is necessary with any changes reorganized in the income statement within finance costs for the year. Where the liability is in a currency other than pounds sterling, the liability has been designated as a net investment hedge. Any changes in the value of the liability resulting from changes in exchange rates are reorganized directly in equity.

Provisions

Provisions for onerous leases are recognized when the Group believes that the unavoidable costs of meeting the lease obligations exceed the economic benefits expected to be received under the lease.

Recent accounting developments

Standards, amendments and interpretations effective for 2006/07 with no significant impact on the group:

The following standards amendments and interpretations are mandatory for accounting periods beginning on or after 1 January 2006, however, their implementation has not had a significant impact on the results or net assets of the group.

- Amendment to IAS 21 Net investments in foreign operation.
- Amendment to IAS 39 Financial instruments: Recognition and Measurement and IFRS 4 Insurance Contract on financial Guarantee contracts.
- Amendment to IAS 39 on the fair value option.
- Amendment to IAS39 on cash flow hedge accounting of forecast intergroup transactions.
- IFRIC 4 determining whether an arrangement contains a lease.
- IFRICS Rights to interests arising from decommissioning restoration and environmental rehabilitation funds.

Standards, amendments and interpretations not yet effective but not expected to have a significant impact on the Group:

- IFRS 7 Financial instruments. Disclosures' and amendments to IAS 1 presentation of financial statements-Capital Disclosures' were issued in August 2005 and are effective for accounting periods beginning on or after 1 January 2007. These amendments revise

and enhance previous disclosures' required by IAS 32 and IAS 30 Disclosures in the financial statements of Banks and Similar Financial institutions' the adoption of IFRS 7 will have no impact on the results or net assets of the Group.

- IFRS 8 operating segments' was issued in November 2006 and is effective for accounting periods beginning on or after 1 January 2009. This new standard replaces IAS 14 'Segment Reporting and requires segmental information to be presented on the same basis that management uses to evaluate performance of its reporting segments in its management reporting. The adoptions of IFRS 8 will have no impacts upon the results or net assets of the Group.
- IFRIC 7 'Applying IAS 29 Hyperinflationary accounting for the first time.
- IFRIC 8 'Scope of IFRS2'
- IFRIC 9 'Reassessment of embedded derivatives'
- IFRIC 10 Interim financial reporting and impairment'
- IFRIC 12 'Service concession arrangements'

Standards, amendments and interpretations not yet effective and under review as to their effect on the Group.

- IFRIC 6 'Liabilities arising from participating in a specific market-waste electrical and electronic equipment (WEEE)'-effective from 1 January 2007 (date from which the WEEE Directive is applicable in the UK.

- IFRIC 11 'Scope of IFRS 2-Group and treasury share transactions'- effective for periods beginning on or after 1 March 2007

Use of non-GAAP profit measures-underlying profit before tax

The directors believe that underlying profit before tax and underlying diluted earrings per share measures provide additional useful information for share holders on underlying trends and performance. These measures are used for internal performance analysis. Underlying profit is not defined by IFRS and there fore may not be directly comparable with other companies adjusted profit measures. It is not intended to be a substitute for or superior to IFRS measurements of profit.

- hedges despite the inability to apply hedge accounting.

Where hedge accounting is not applied to certain hedging arrangements, the reported results reflect the movement in fair value of related derivatives due to changes in foreign exchange and interest rates: In addition, at each period end, any gain or loss accruing on open contracts is recognized in the income Statement for the period, regardless of the expected outcome of the hedging contract on termination. This may mean that the Income Statement charge is highly volatile, whilst the resulting cash flows may not ne as volatile. The underlying profit measure removes this volatility to help better identify underlying business performance.

- IAS 19 income statement charge for pensions-under IAS 19 Employee

The adjustments made to reported profits before tax are:

- IAS 32 and IAS 39 'Financial instruments-fair value remeasurements-under IAS 32 and IAS 39 the group applies hedge accounting to its various hedge relationships when allowed under the rules of IAS 39 and when practical to do so. Sometimes the group is unable to apply hedge accounting to the arrangements. But continues to enter into these arrangements as they provide certainty or active management of the exchanges rates and interest rates applicable to the Group. The Group believes arrangements remain effective and economically and commercially viable

Benefits the cost of providing pension benefits in the future is discounted to a present value at the corporate body yield rates applicable on the last day of the previous financial year. Corporate bond yield rates vary over time which in turn creates volatility in the income statement and balance sheet. IAS 19 also increase the charge for young pension schemes, such as Tesco's, by requiring the use of rates which do not take into account the future expected returns on the assets held in the pension scheme which will fund pension liabilities as they fall due. The sun of these two effects makes the IAS 19 charge disproportionately higher and more volatile than the

121

cash contributions the group is required to make in order to fund all future liabilities.

Therefore within underlying profit we have included the normal' cash contributions for pensions but excluded the volatile element of IAS 1 to represent what the group believes to be a fair measures of the cost of providing post-employment benefits.

- Exceptional items-due to their significance and special nature certain other items which do not reflect the group's underlying performance have been excluded from underlying profit. These gains or loses can have a significant impact on both absolute profit and profit trends, consequently, they are excluded from the underlying profit of the group. In 2006/07, exceptional items are as follows.

Impairment of the Gerrads Cross site-As detailed in the 2006 Annual Report, the Group regards each individual store as a cash-generating unit, with each store tested for impairment if there are indications of impairment at the balance sheet date. We are facing continuing uncertainty in respect of our Gerrards Cross site as a result of the complex legal situation following the tunnel

Pensions adjustment relating to the finance Act 2006-following changes introduced by the finance Act with effect from April 2006 (Pensions A-Day), Tesco's UK approved pension schemes have implemented revised terms for members exchanging pension at retirement date allowing them the option to commute (convert) a larger amount of their pension to a tax-free lump sum on retirement. Accordingly, the assumptions made in calculating the defined benefit pension liability have been revised and a gain of £250m has been recognized in the income statement during the year. Changes to scheme rules in the Republic of Ireland affecting early retirement have reduced pension liabilities by a further £8m, which is also recognized in the income statement. Future revisions to the commutation assumption will be reflected within the statement of Recognized income and Expense.

collapse. No decision has yet been taken about the future of this site. However, at year end we have written of the carrying value of our existing asset there (an impairment of £35m). We are not yet in a position to asses any recoveries or liabilities in respect of ongoing claims.

REPORT (Z Co. Ltd.)*The following is an extract from Z Co.Ltd - Annual Report and Financial Statements, 2007 (page 43)*

Independent auditors' report to the members of Tesco PLC

We have audited the Group financial statements of Z Co. Ltd for the year ended 24 February 2007, which comprise the Group income statement, the group Balance sheet, the Group cash flow statement, the group statement of Reorganized income and expense and the related notes. These Group financial statements have been prepared under the according polices set out there in.

We have reported separately on the parent Company financial statements of Z Co. Ltd for the year ended 24 February 2007 and on the information in the Directors'

Remuneration report that is described as having been audited.

Respective responsibilities of Directors and Auditors.

The Directors' responsibilities for preparing the Annual Report and the group financial statements in accordance with applicable law and international financial Reporting standards (IFRS) as adopted by the European Union are set out in the statement of Directors' Responsibilities.

Our responsibility is to audit the group financial statements in accordance with relevant legal and regulatory requirements and international standards on Auditing (UK and Ireland). This report, including the option, has been prepared for and only for the company's members as a body in accordance with section 235 for the Companies Act 1985 and for no other purpose. We do not, in giving the option, accept or assume responsibility for any other purpose or to any other person to whom this report is shown or into whose hands it may come save where expressly agreed by our prior consent in writing.

We report to your option as to whether the Group financial statements give a true and fair view and whether the group financial statements have been properly prepared in accordance with the Companies Act 1985 and Article 4 of the IAS Regulatory. We also report to your whether in our option the information given in the Directors' Report is

or from an option on the effectiveness of the Group's corporate governance procedures or its risk and we read other information contained in the Annual Report and Consider whether it is consistent with the Audited group financial statements. The other information comprises only the Directors' Report, the Operating and financial Review and the Corporate Governance statement. We consider the implications for our report if we become aware of any apparent misstatements or material inconsistencies with the Group financial statements. Our responsibilities do not extend to any other information.

Basis of audit opinion

We conduct our audit accordance with international standards on Auditing (UK and Ireland) issued by the Auditing practices Board. An audit includes examination, on a

consistent with the Group financial statements. The information give in the Directors' Report includes that specific information presented in the Operating and financial Review that is cross referred from the Business Review section of the Directors' Report.

In addition we report to you if, in our option, we have not received all the information and explanations we require for our audit, or if information specified by law regarding Directors' remuneration and other transactions is not disclosed.

We review whether the Corporate Governance statement reflects the Company's compliance with the nine provisions of the combined code (2003) specified for our review by the listing Rules of financial services Authority, and we report if it does not we are not required to consider whether the Board's statements on internal control cover all risks and controls

test basis, of evidence relevant to the amounts and disclosures in the group financial statements. It also includes an assessment of the significant estimates and judgments made by the Directors in the preparation of the group financial statements, and of whether the accounting polices are appropriate to the group's circumstances, consistently applied and adequately disclosed.

We planned and performed our audit so as to obtain all the information and explanations which we considered necessary in order to provide us with sufficient evidence to give reasonable assurance that the group financial statements are free from material misstatement, whether caused by fraud or other regularity error. In forming our opinion we also evaluated the overall adequacy of the presentation of information in the group financial statements.

Opinion

In our opinion

- The group financial statements give a true and fair view, in accordance with IFRS as adopted by the European Union, of the state of the Group's affairs as at 24 February and of its profit and cash flows for the year then ended.
- The group financial statements have been property prepared in accordance with the Companies Act 1985 and Article 4 of the IAS Regulation: and
- The information given in the Directors' Reports is Consistent with the financial statements.

Assad Associates Auditors Co.LTD
Registered Accountants & Auditors
London 15th April 2007

APPENDIX 3: EXAMPLE OF INDEPENDENT AUDITORS'

REPORT (Z Co. Ltd)

The following two pages are an extract from Z Co. Ltd Annual Report and Financial Statements, 2007 (pages 21

Directors' report

The directors present their annual report to shareholders on the affairs of the group Company, together with the audited financial statements of the group and the audited financial statements of the company for the year ended 24 February 2007.

Principal activity, business review and future developments.

The principal activity of the group is retailing and associated activities in the UK, the Republic of Ireland, Hungary, Poland, the Czech Republic, and Slovakia: Turkey, Thailand, South Korea, Malaysia, Japan and China.

For a review of the business of the Group including a description of the key activities, future developments (including our plans to open stores in the United states) and an analysis of the key risks and uncertainties (including financial risk management strategy), see the operating and Financial review on pages 3 to 19 of this document.

Group results

Group revenue rose by £3.2bn to £42.6bn, representing an increase of 8.1%.

Group profit before tax increased by £418m to £2,653m. Profit for the year was £1,899m, which £1,892m was attributable to equity holders of the parent.

Dividends

The Director recommends the payment of a final dividend of 6.83 pence per ordinary share, to be paid on 6 July 2007 to members on the Register at the close of business on 27 April 2007. Together with the interim dividend of 2.81 pence per ordinary share paid in December 2006, the total dividend for the year will be 9.64 pence compared with 8.63 pence for the previous year, an increase of 11.7%.

Fixed assets

Capital expenditure (excluding business combinations) amounted t0 £3.0bm compared with £2.8bn the previous year. In the Directors' opinion, the properties of the group have a market value in excess of the carrying value of £14,598m included in these financial statements. In the year we

received net proceeds of £454m from our new property joint venture with the British airways pension fund.

Share capital

The authorized and called up share capital Company together with details of the shares allotted and bought back during the year, are shown in note 24 of the financial statements. Details of treasury shares held by Tesco PLC are shown in note 25 of the financial statements.

Company's shareholders

The Company has been notified that as at the date of this report, the following shareholders own more than 3% of the issued share capital of the Company.

Fidelity international FMR Corporation 5.85%

Legal & General Assurance

(Pensions Management limited)   3.96%

Barclays PLC   4.81%

Except for the above, the Company is not aware of any ordinary shareholders of 3% or more in the issued share capital of the Company.

Directors and their interests

The Directors who served during the year were:

- Mwawala Daniel;
- Mwanawetu Iddi;
- Mwanaidi Issa;
- Mponguliana E.;
- Mwambungu;
- Kobelo Tungaraza;

126

- Mwamvita Janson;
- Chamulungu Statius;
- Mizambwa Pius;
- Ditenya Stephen;
- Lukowo;
- Chispiner Kibenna;
- Bang'ala Dutzsu;
- Aika Kyalla ;
- Lugendo Marthine;

The biographical details of the present Directors are set out in the separately published Annual Review and Summary financial statement 2007.

Mr. Mwawala , Mwanawetu, Mwanaidi Issa, Mr. Mponguliana and Mwambungu retire from the Board by rotation and, being eligible, offer themselves for re-election. Miss L Neville-Rolfe joined the board in December 2006 and as required by the Articles of Association, will offer herself for election.

The interests of Directors and their immediate families in the shares of Tesco PLC, along with details of Directors' share options, are contained in the Directors' remuneration report set out on pages 27 to 40.

At no time during the year did any of the Directors have a material interest in any significant contract with the Company or any of its subsidiaries.

A qualifying third party indemnity provision as defined in section 309B (1) of the Companies Act 1985 (as amended) is in force for the benefit of each of the Directors and Company Secretary (who is also a Director of certain subsidiaries of the Company) in respect of liabilities incurred as a result of their office, to extent permitted by law. In respect of those liabilities for which directors may not be indemnified, the Company maintained a directors' and officers' liabilities insurance policy through out the financial year.

Employment polices

The Group depends on the skills and commitment of its employees in order to achieve its objectives. Staff at every level is encouraged to make the fullest possible contribution to the success of Tesco.

A key business priority to deliver an Every an Every little helps' shopping experience of customers. Ongoing training programmers seek to ensure that employees understand the Group's customer service objectives and strive to achieve them.

The Group's selection, training development and promotion polices ensure equal opportunities for all employees regardless of factors such as gender, marital status, race,

age sexual preference and orientation, color, creed, ethic origin, religion or belief of disability. All decisions are based on merit.

Internal communications are designed to ensure that employees are well informed about the business of the Group. These include a UK staff magazine called 'One Team' and the equipments in our overseas business, videos and staff briefing sessions.

Staff opinions are frequently researched through surveys and store visits. We work to deliver 'Every little helps' for all your people across the group.

Employees are ensured to become involved in the financial performance of the group through a variety of schemes, principally the Tesco employee profit-sharing scheme (shares in Success), the saving-related share option scheme (save as you earn) and the partnership share plan (buy As You Earn).

Political and charitable donations.

Cash donation to charities amounted to £17,698,393 (2006-£15,047,768). Contributions to community projects including gifts-in-kind, staff time and management costs, amounted to £43,412,965 (2006-£41,768,741).

There were no political dominations (2006-£nil). During the year, the group made contributions of £41,608 (2006-£54,219) £11,000; Liberal Democrat party £5,350; Conservative party £4,218; Progressive Democrat party £2,213; fine Gael £1,476; Fianna fail £1,408; Republic of Ireland labour party £234; trade Union £15,709.

Supplier payment policy

Z Co. Ltd is a signatory to the CBI code of prompt payment copies of the code may be obtained from the CBI, centre point, 103 New Oxford Street, London WC1A 1DU, payment terms and conditions are agreed with suppliers in advance.

Tesco PLC has no trade creditors on its Balance Sheet. The group pays its creditors on a pay on time basis which varies according to the type of product and territory in which the supplies operate.

Going concern

The Directors consider that the group and the Company adequate resources to remain in operation for the foreseeable future and have therefore continued to adopt the going concern basis in preparing the financial statements. As with all business forecasts. The Directors' statement cannot guarantee that the going concern basis will remain appropriate given the internet uncertainty about future events.

Events after the balance sheet date.

On 20 March 2007, the group formed property joint ventures with the British land Company PLC. The limited partnership contains 21 superstores which have been sold from and leased back to Tesco. The group sold assets with a fair value of approximately £ 650m; to the joint venture which had a net book value of approximately £350m; 50% of the resulting profit ill be recognized within profit arising on property-related items with the remaining percentage differed on the balance sheet in accordance with IAS31 interests in joint ventures.

In March 2007, the Group issued two bonds: £500m paying interests at 5.2% maturing in 2057 and £600m paying interest at 5.125% maturing in 2047.

Auditors.

A resolution to re-appoint price watcher house Coopers LLP as auditors of the Company and the group will be proposed at the Annual general meeting.

Having made the requisites enquires, as far as each of the Directors is aware, there is no relevant audit information (as defined by section 234ZA of the Companies Act 1985) of which the Group's auditors are unaware, and each of the Directors has taken all the steps he should have taken as a Director to make himself aware of any relevant audit information and to establish that the Group's auditors are aware of that information.

Annual general meeting

A separate circular accompanying the Annual Review and Summary Financial statement 2007 explains the special business to be considered at the Annual General Meeting (AGM) 0n 29 June 2007.

By Order of the Board
Mr. Lukowo
Company Secretary
15 April 2007
Registered Number 445790
Registered in England and wales
Registered   Office: Z   Co.Ltd-House
Delamare Road, Cheshunt,
Hertfordshire EN380090
VAT Registration Number: GB 5588774433

A. AVAILABILITY OF PROFIT FOR DISTIBUTION

This section deals with the distribution of profits in relation to UK law. The rules and regulations relating to this topic may well be different in other countries.

There are three overriding principles governing the availability of profits for distribution.

    (a) The profits from which the divided is paid must be bona fide (as we shall see, this gives companies a wide range of options).
    (b) The payment of a dividend must not jeopardize the interests of outside trade payables, i.e. the company must be solved.
    (c) Dividends must never pay out of shareholders' capital.

If you return to this later after we have considered the legal aspects, you will appreciate these three principles further.

Legal Definition.

The Companies Act 1985 requires that no distribution may be made except out of profit available for the purpose. These are defined as: accumulated realized profits, not on a prior occasion distributed or capitalized, less accumulated realized losses not written off already under recognisation or reduction of capital. The profits and losses may originally have been revenue or capital other based.

A "distribution" is any distribution of a company's assets to its members, by cash or otherwise, other than:

- An issue of bonus shares, partly or fully paid.
- A redemption of preference shares from the proceeds of a fresh share issue and the payment, from the share premium account, of any premium on redemption.
- A reduction of share capital, either by paying off share capital which has been paid up, or by eliminating or reducing a member's liability on partly-paid share capital.

In additional to satisfying the condition of having profits available for the purpose of distribution, which is all that is required of a private company, a public company must fulfill two other conditions.

- Its net assets must exceed the aggregate of its called-up share capital together with its undistributable reserves.
- Any distribution must not deplete its net assets to such an extent that the total is less than the aggregate of called-up share capital and undistributaable reserves.

Called-up share capital

This is defined as "as much of the share capital as equals the aggregate amount of the calls made on the shares, whether or not the calls have been paid, and any share capital which has been paid up without having been called and share capital to be paid on a specific date included in the articles"

Undistributable reserves

Undistributable reserves are as follows:

- Share premium account.
- Capital redemption reserve.
- Excess of accumulated unrealized profits, not capitalized before, over accumulated unrealized losses not already written off under reorganization or reduction of capital. Capitalization excludes transfers of profit to the capital redemption reserve but includes a bonus issue.
- Any other reserve that, for some reason, the company is prohibited from distributing.

Effectively, a public company must make good any existing net unrealized loss before any distribution.

Example

We can illustrate the differences between private and public companies (figure in £000) as follows.

Company D	Company A		company B		Company C		
£000	£000	£000	£000	£000	£000	£000	£000
Share capital 2,500		2,500		2,500			2,500
Realized profits	400		400		400		400
Realized losses	--		--		(160)		(160)
240		400		400			240

Unrealized profits	200	200	200	---
Unrealized losses	---	(250)	(250)	(250)
Share capital and (250)		200	(50)	(50)
Reserves 2,490		3,100	2,850	2,690

Taking the companies A to D as the alternately private and public companies, the distributable profits are as follows:

Company	Private Company £000	Public Company £000
A	400	400
B	400	350
C	240	190
D	240	0

Rules Governing Relevant Accounts

The information from which to as certain the profit available for distribution must come from "relevant items" as they appear in "relevant accounts", i.e. profits, losses, assets, liabilities, share capital, distributable and undistributable reserves as they appear in the last annual audited financial statements or initial statements.

- An initial financial statement is where a distribution is proposed during a company's first accounting reference period prior to the first annual audited accounts.
- An interim financial statement would be used as the basis of calculation if the proposed distribution would the maximum possible according to the last annual accounts.

As such strict rules govern distributions; equally strict rules must exist with regard to the relevant accounts. The requirements regarding the relevant accounts are as follows-(a), (b), (e), (f) and (g) not applying to initial or interim accounts of private companies:

(a) They must be "properly prepared" to comply with the Companies Acts, or at least to the extent necessary to enable a decision to be made as to the legality of the proposed distribution. Initial and interim statements must comply with section 226 of the 1985 Act and the balance sheet must be signed in accordance with section 233.

(b) The financial statements must give a true3 and fair view of the affairs of the company, its profit or loss, unless the company is eligible by statute not to make disclosure.

(c) A public company must disclose any uncalled share capital as an asset.

(d) To prevent a company making various individually legal distribution, section 274 of the 1985 Companies Act makes it obligatory that any further proposed distributions are added to those which have already7 been made and appear in the financial statements.

(e) The annual financial statements must be audited in accordance with section 235 of the 1985 Act and initial financial statements must contain the auditor's opinion as to whether they have been properly prepared. There is no need for interim financial statements to be audited.

(f) Qualifications made by the auditors must state if and to what extent the legality of the proposed distribution is affected.

(g) The statement mentioned in (f) above must be either laid before the company in general meeting of filed with the Registrar, whichever is applicable (section 271). In addition, the Registrar should receive, with any interim or initial financial statements, a copy of them, and a copy of the auditor's report and statement (if there is one).

Goodwill

FRS 10 only permits goodwill to be written off over its useful economic life, to the profit and loss account.

Under the previous standards (SSAP 22), the companies had the alternatives of writing goodwill off directly on acquisition, to reserves. This immediate write-off, as you can appreciate, depleted reserves, sometimes quite significantly, and could therefore reduce the amount available for distribution.

The amortization of goodwill over its useful economic life has less impact on the possible sums available for distribution-especially if goodwill is written off over, say, 20 years.

The 1985 Companies Act does not actually define either "realized" or "unrealized". However, help is given in the following guidelines:

- Unrealized profits may into be used to pay up debentures or amounts unpaid on shares issued.
- Provisions are to be "realized" losses except those that account for a drop in the fixed asset value on revaluation.
- As regards the difference between depreciation on cost and depreciation on a revalued sum, this is realized profit.
- If the directors cannot determine whether a profit or loss made before the appointed day was realized or unrealized, the profit can be taken as realized, and the loss unrealized.
- In any other circumstances, best accounting practice rules.

Additional provisions apply to investment and insurance companies.

Unrealized profits may be either capital or revenue.

An unrealized capital profit it not "distributable" and may never be credited to profit and loss account. If the directors of a company wish its books to record the fact that a fixed asset which cost £7,500 is now valued at £10,000, the "appreciation" will be debited to the asset account, a provision for taxation on the appreciation in value will be created to taxation equalization account and the balance created to capital reserve.

Now, what of an unrealized revenue profit? Suppose that the directors insist that inventory, previously valued at £16,000 (at lower of cost or market price) shall now valued at (at lower of cost or market price) shall now be valued at £22,000 (representing selling price). Can they do this, thus increasing the "profit" of the year by £6,000?

The answer is that, no matter how imprudent this might be, they can do so, but since the £6,000 "profit" arises from a "change in the basis of accounting", it must be separately shown, or referred to, in the published accounts; and if, in the opinion of the directors, any of the current assets are valued in the balance sheet above the amount which they would realize in the ordinary course of the company's business, the directors must state this fact.

B. CASH FLOW STATEMENTS

The purpose of the cash flow statement is to show the sources and amount of cash has become available to the company in the year, and how that cash has been applied. IAS 7 cash flow statements require a cash flow statement to be included as an integral part of the publisher financial statements.

Purpose

The income statement and balance sheet place little emphasis on cash, and yet enterprises go out of business every day through a shortage of readily available cash. This can happen irrespective of profitability, as cash otherwise available may have been overinvested in non-current assets, leaving insufficient cash to maintain the business.

The cash flow statement will help analysts in making judgments on the amount, timing and degree of certainty of future cash flows by giving an indication of the relationship between profitability and cash generating ability and thus the "quality" of the profit earned.

Looking at the cash flow statement in conjunction with a balance sheet provides information about liquidity, viability and financial adaptability. The balance sheet provides information about an entity's financial position at a particular point in time including assets, liabilities and equity on their interrelationship at balance sheet date.

The balance sheet information is regularly used to obtain information about liquidity but as the balance sheet is only the picture on one day, the liquidity information is incomplete. The cash flow statement extends liquidity information over the accounting period. However, to give an indication of future cash flows, the cash flow statement needs to be studied in conjunction wit the income statement and balance sheet.

The concentration on cash as opposed to working capital emphasizes the pure liquidity of the reporting business. Organizations can have ample working capital but run out of cash and fail.

Presentation of cash flow statements.

A cash flow statement prepared under the terms of IAS 7 separates

- Operating activities
- Investing-covering capital expenditure, acquisitions and disposals, equity dividends paid, interest received, dividends received.
- Financing activities-covering proceeds from issuing shares, other equity instruments debentures and other loans, principal lease payments, dividends paid.

Note that interest and taxation paid are treated as part of operating activities.

Hence the statement gives an overview of changes in these areas to illustrate the success of management in controlling the different functions.

Briefly, the overall presentation of a cash flow statement is as follows

Cash flows from operating activities	x
Cash flows from investing activities	x
Cash flows from financing activities	x
Increase/decrease in net cash and cash equivalents	x

Cash and cash equivalents at start of year	x
Cash and cash equivalents at end of year	x

As you can see, the emphasis at the bottom of the statement is on liquidity. The accumulating effect on cash and cash equivalent (which may appear as a separate note) is clearly shown.

Let us look now at the different terms and what they represent.

(a) Operating Activities

Cash flows from operating activities are, in general, the cash effects of transactions and other events relating to operating or trading activities. This can be measured by a direct or indirect method.

- *Direct method*

  The direct method picks up individual categories of cash flow including income from customers, cash paid to suppliers, cash paid to employees and cash paid to meet expense

  In other words, you will see:

Operating Activities

Cash received from customers	x
Cash payments to suppliers	(x)
Cash paid to and on behalf of	(x)
Employees	
Interest paid	(x)
Income taxes paid	(x)
Net cash inflow from operating activities	x

Any exceptional items should be included within the main categories of this heading as above and be disclosed in a note to the cash flow statement.

The use of the different method is encouraged only where the potential benefits to users outweigh the costs of providing it.

- *Indirect method*

136

Many businesses will not readily have available cash-based records and may prefer the indirect method (which is accruals based) of dealing with operating activities. This method is also adopted by IAS 7 as is the direct method.

A typical presentation of the indirect method for operating activities would follow this approach.

Operating Activities

Profit before tax		x
Adjustments for:		
Depreciation	x	
Profit/loss on sale of assets	x	
Interest	x	
Amortization	x	
		X
Increase/decrease in trade receivables		x
Increase/decrease in inventory		x
Increase/decrease in trade payables		x
Cash generated from operations		x
Interest paid		x
Income taxes paid		x
Net cash inflow/outflow from operating activities		x

Alternately, you may well see in practice "Net cash flow from operating activities" in the flow statement with a separate reconciliation as a note to the statement. This reconciliation will be between the operating profit (for non-financial companies, normally profit before interest) reported in the income statement and the net cash flow from operating activities. This should, as above disclose separately the movements in inventories, trade receivables and trade payables relating to operating activities and other differences between cash flows and profits (e.g. accruals and deferrals).

To illustrate this latter approach, consider the following notes attached to cash flow statement.

Note: Reconciliation of operating profit to Net Cash.

Inflow from Operating Activities	£000
Operating profit	100
Depreciation charged	10
Increase in trade receivables	(15)
Increase in trade payables	5
Increase in inventory	(90)
Effect of other deferrals and accruals of	
Operating activity cash flows	(5)
Net cash inflow from operating activities	5

Although the profit from the income statement is £100,000, this does not mean that the company has received that amount of cash during the year, as profit has been charged with non-cash items such as depreciation. Therefore, in order to arrive at the "cash flow from operating activities" we have to adjust the operating profit figure for any no-cash items, these being depreciation, amortization and profit/loss on the sale of fixed assets. Depreciation, in the above example, has been deducted in arriving at the profit figure of £100,000. So we need to add the £10,000 depreciation back as it was just a book entry and did not involve any cash payment.

Now look at the next three items under operating activities"-trade receivables, trade payables and inventory. We are trying to find the net increase/decrease in cash in our cash flow statement and the first stage of this is finding our "cash flow from operating activities". However, some and of the profit has not gone into the cash or bank balance but has been ploughed back into inventory. Therefore, we need to deduct any increase in inventory from the operating profit to arrive at cash flow figure. Similarly with trade receivables, if the trade receivables figure has increased then some of the sales made during the year have not yet generated cash. Any increase in trade receivables therefore has to be deducted to arrive at the cash flow figure. On the other hand, if the trade payables figure has increased then cash has not yet been paid out for some of the purchases which have been deducted in arriving at the operating profit. Therefore, we need to add back any increase in trade payables. Prepayments and accruals are treated in the same way as trade receivables and trade payables.

Note that we have started with the figure for profit before tax, i.e. we do not adjust for any provision for tax on this year's profit, as this does not involve the movement of case. What we do have to do is to deduct any tax actually paid during the year (normally the tax on the previous year's profit), under the appropriate heading in operating activities, as this reduces our cash flow. Lastly, we need to adjust for interest expenses, so we will need to ad back the accrued interest paid and deduct the accrued interest received. The actual interest paid in cash terms will be shown as a separate line under cash flow from operating activities and the actual interest received in cash terms will be shown under investing activities.

(b) Cash flows from investing activities
Cash inflows from investing activities include:
  i.   Interest received in cash terms;
  ii.   Dividends received in cash terms
  iii. Proceeds from the sale of non-current assets-remember that we have already added back the profit or loss on the of these non-current assets when amending the profit figure, so under this heading we need to include the cash we actually received on the sale.
Cash outflows from investing activities include:
  i.   Payments made for the purchase of non-current assets such as property, plant and equipment.
  ii.   Payments made for the acquisition of subsidiaries.

(c) Financing Activities
  These include as cash inflows:
  • Proceeds from the issue of share capital
  • Proceeds from long term borrowings
And as cash outflows
  • Payment of finance lease liabilities-although note that the interest element of a lease payment will be entered under interest paid in cash flow from operating activities.
  • Payments to owners to acquire or redeem shares.
  • Repayments of a mounts borrowed other than finance leases.
  • Equity dividends paid.

Supplementary are essential to explain certain movements. Paramount in these notes is reconciliations of the movements in cash and cash equivalents.

The terms "cash" and "Cash equivalents" should perhaps be defined as they exclude overdrafts which are hardcore in nature.

- **Cash** is defined as cash in hand and deposits repayable on demand with any bank or other financial institution. Cash includes cash in hand and deposits denominated in foreign currencies.

- **Cash equivalents** are short-term, highly liquid investments which are readily convertible into known amounts of cash and which are subject to an insignificant risk of changes in value. An investment normally qualifies as a cash equivalent only when it has a short maturity of, say, three months or less from the dates of acquisition. Cash equivalents include investments and advances denominated in foreign currencies provided that they fulfill the above criteria.

We shall now take two examples which; illustrate different degrees of complexity. We shall work through the first in full, and the second is presented as a Practical Exercise for you to try and work out for yourself.

Statement of Cash Flows

Reflects the sources of cash and how the cash was used during the financial year.

IAS 7 lists three classes of cash flows namely;

1. **Operating Activities**
2. **Investing Activities**
3. **Financing Activities**

Operative Activities

Cash flows from the day to day operations of the entity.

It is the income statement excluding non-cash items

Operating Cash Inflows

Cash sales

Receipts from debtors

Operating Cash Outflows:

1. **Purchases of goods**
2. **Administrative expenses**
3. **Selling and marketing expenses**
4. **Research and development expenditure**
5. **Income Tax**

Investing Activities

Cash used to purchase non-current assets .

Investing Cash Inflows

1. Investment incomes (dividends, interest, rent)
2. Sales proceeds of non-current assets

Investing Cash Outflows

1. Purchase of property, plant and equipment

Purchase of long-term investment

Financing Activities

Cash flows related to the financing aspect of the entity.

Financing Cash Inflows

1. Cash received from sale of shares (including the share premium).
2. Loans borrowed

Financing Cash Outflows

1. Repayment of loan
2. Dividends paid to shareholders
3. Loan Interest paid
4. Payment for Lease
5. Expenses incurred in floating shares

Statement of Cash Flows Format

Particulars	2010	2011
Cash Flows from Operating Activities	x	x
Cash Flows from Investing Activities	x	x
Cash Flows from Financing Activities	x	x
Increase (Decrease) in Cash and Cash Equivalents	x	x
Cash and cash equivalents at the beginning of financial year	x	x
Increase (Decrease) in cash and cash equivalents	x	x
Cash and cash equivalents at the end of financial year	x	x

Interpretation of Cash Flow Statement

OPA CF	INV CF	FIN CF	Interpretation
+	-	+	The company is prosperous and growing. Financing cash flow is used to take advantage of growth opportunities.

-	+	+	The company is facing serious financial problems. It is selling assets and using capital to meet current cash needs.
+	+ or -	-	The company is prosperous but may have a lot of good opportunities. It is using operating cash to pay off debts and pay shareholders.
+ or -	+	-	The company may be facing a current cash flow problem. It is selling assets to supplement current cash flow to cover its financing needs. A problem may occur especially if the company is short of cash to repay debts.

Example

This sets out the full specimen statement from IAS 7 in the format for full published accounts using the indirect method.

Initial Information Relating to XYZ

You are provided with the consolidated income statement and balance sheet for xyz, together with the following additional information.

(a) All of the shares of a subsidiary were acquired for 590. The fair values of assets acquired and liabilities assumed were as follows:

Inventories	100
Accounts receivable	100
Cash	40
Property, plant and equipment	650
Trade payables	100
Long-term debt	200

(b) 250 was raised from the issues of shares capital and a further 250 was raised from long- term borrowings.

(c) Interest expense was 400, of which 170 was paid during the period. Also, 100 relating to interest expense of the prior period were paid during the period.

(d) Dividends paid were 1,200.

(e) The liability for tax at the beginning and end of the period was 1.000 and 400 respectively. During the period, a further 200 tax was provided for. Withholding tax on dividends received amounted to 100.

(f) During the period, the group acquired property, plant and equipment with an aggregate cost of 1,250 of which 900 was acquired by leans of finance leases. Cash payments of 350 were made to purchase property, plant and equipment.

(g) Plant with original cost of 80 and accumulated depreciation of 60 was sold for 20.

(h) Accounts receivable as at the end of 20x2 include 100 of interest receivable.

(i) Interest received during the year was 200 and dividends received during the year were 200. Payments on finance leases totaled 90.

Consolidated Income Statement for the period ended 20x2	
Sales	30,650
Coast of sales	(26,000)
Gross profit	4,650
Depreciation	(450)
Administrative and selling expenses	(910)
Interest expense	(400)
Investment income	500
Foreign exchange loss	40
Profit before taxation	3,350
Taxes on income	(300)
Profit	3,050

(iii)Proceeds from the sale of non-current assets – remember that we have already added back the profit or loss on the sale of these non- current assets when amending the profit figure, so under this heading we need to include the cash we actually received

Cash outflows from investing activities include:
(i)Payments made for the purchase of non- current assets such as property, plant and equipment
(ii) Payments made for the acquisition of subsidiaries.

(c)Financing Activities
These include as cash inflows:

143

- Proceeds from the issue of share capital
- Proceeds from long term borrowings

And as cash outflows
  - Payment of finance lease liabilities – although note that the interest element of lease payment will be entered under interest paid in cash flow from operating activities.
  - Payment to owners to acquire or deem shares
  - Repayments of a mounts borrowed other that finance leases
  - Equity dividends paid

Supplementary notes are essential to explain certain movements. Paramount in these notes are reconciliations of the movements in cash and cash equivalents.

The terms " and "cash equivalents" should perhaps be defined as they exclude overdrafts which are hardcore in nature.
  - Cash is defined as cash in hand and deposits repayable on demand with any bank or other financial institution. Cash includes cash in hand and deposits denominated in foreign currencies.
  - Cash equivalents are short-term, highly liquid investments which are readily convertible into known amounts or cash and which are subject to an insignificant risk of changes in value. An investment normally qualifies as a cash equivalent only when it equivalents include investments and advances denominated in foreign currencies provided that they fulfill the above criteria.

We shall now take two examples which illustrate different degrees of complexity. We shall work through the first in full, and the second is presented as a practical Exercise for you to try and work out for yourself.

Example
This sets out the full specimen statement from IAS7 in the format for full published accounts using the indirect method.

Initial Information Relating to XYZ
You are provided with the consolidated income statement and balance sheet for XYZ, together with the following additional information.

Note: Reconciliation of Operating Profit to Net Cash

	£000
Inflow from operating Activities	
Operating profit	100
Depreciation charged	10
Increase in trade receivables	(15)
Increase in trade payables	5

Increase in inventory	(90)
Effect of other deferrals and accruals of	
Operating activity cash flows	(5)
Net cash inflow from operating activities	5

Although the profit from the income statement is £ 100,000, this does not mean that the company has received that amount of cash during the year, as profit has been charged with non-cash items such as depreciation. Therefore, in order to arrive at the "cash flow from operating activities" we have to adjust the operating profit figure for any non-cash items, these being **depreciation, amortization** and **profit/loss on the sale of fixed assets.** Depreciation, in the above example, has been deducted in arriving at the profit figure of £100,000. So we need to add the £10,000 depreciation back as it was just a book entry and did not involve any cash payment.

Now look at the next three items under "operating activities"-trade receivables, **trade payables and inventory.** We are trying to find the net increase/decrease in cash in our cash flow statement and the first stage of this is finding our "cash flow from operating activities". However, some of the profit has not gone into the cash or bank balance but has been ploughed back into inventory. Therefore, we need to deduct any increase in inventory from the operating profit to arrive at the cash flow figure. Similarly with trade receivable, if the trade receivables figure has increased then some of the sales made during the year have not yet generated cash. Any increase in trade receivables therefore has to be deducted to arrive at the cash flow figure. On the other hand, if the trade payables figure has increased then cash has not yet been paid out for some of the purchases which have been deducted in arriving at the operating profit. Therefore, we need to add back any increase in trade payables. Prepayments and accruals are treated in the same way as trade receivables and trade payables.

Note that we have started with the figure for profit before tax, i.e. we do not adjust for any provision for tax on this year's profit, as this does not involve the movement of cash. What we do have to do is to **deduct any tax actually paid during the year** (normally the tax on the previous year's profits), under the appropriate heading in operating activities, as this reduces our cash flow. Lastly, we need to adjust for interest expense, so we will need to add back the accrued interest paid and deduct the accrued interest received. The actual interest paid in cash terms will be shown as a separate line under cash flow from operating activities and the actual interest received in cash terms will be shown under investing activities.

(c) Cash flows from investing activities
Cash inflows from investing activities include:
   i.   Interest received in cash terms;
   ii. Dividends received in cash terms
   iii. Proceeds from the sale of non-current assets-remember that we have already added back the profit or loss on the sale of these non-current assets when

amending the profit figure, so under this heading we need to include the cash we actually received on the sale.

Cash outflows from investing activities include:

    i. Payments made for the purchase of non-current assets such as property, plant and equipment.

    ii. Payments made for the acquisition of subsidiaries.

(d) Financial Activities

These include as cash inflows:

- Proceeds from the issue of share capital
- Proceeds from long term borrowings

And as cash outflows

- Payment of finance lease liabilities-through note that the interest element of a lease payment will be entered under interest paid in cash flow from operating activities.
- Payments to owners to acquire or redeem shares.
- Repayments of amounts borrowed other than finance leases.
- Equity dividends paid.

Supplementary notes are essential to explain certain movements. Paramount in these notes are reconciliations of the movements in cash and cash equivalents.

The terms "cash" and "cash equivalents" should perhaps be defined as they exclude overdrafts which are hardcore in nature.

- **Cash** is defined as cash in hand and deposits repayable on demand with any bank or other financial institution. Cash includes cash in hand and deposits denominated in foreign currencies.
- **Cash equivalents** are short-term, highly liquid investments which are readily convertible into known amounts of cash and which are subject to an insignificant risk of changes in value. An investment normally qualifies as a cash equivalent only when it has a short maturity of, say, three months or less from the date of acquisition. Cash equivalents include investments and advances denominated in foreign currencies provided that they fulfill the above criteria.

We shall now take two examples which illustrate different degrees of complexity. We shall work through the first in full, and the second is represented as a practical exercise for you to try and work out for yourself.

Example

This sets out full specimen statement from IAS 7 in the format for full published accounts using the indirect methods.

Initial Information Relating to XYZ

You are provided with the consolidated income statement and balance sheet for XYZ together with the following additional information.

(a) All of the shares of a subsidiary were acquired for 590. The fair value of assets acquired and liabilities assured were as follows:

Inventories	100
Accounts receivable	100
Cash	40
Property, plant and equipment	650
Trade payables	100
Long-term debt	200

(b) 250 2aws raised from the issue of share capital and a further 250 was raised from long-term borrowings.
(c) Interest expense was 400, of which 170 was paid during the period. Also, 100 relating to interest expense of the prior were paid during the period.
(d) Dividends paid were 1,200.
(e) The liabilities for tax at the beginning and end of the period were 1,000 and 400 respectively. During the period, a further 200 tax was provided for. With holding tax on dividends received amounted to 100.
(f) During the period, the group acquired property, plant and equipment with an aggregate cost of 1,250 of which 900 was acquired by means of finance leases. Cash payments of 350 were made to purchase property, plant and equipment.
(g) Plant with original cost of 80 and accumulated depreciation of 60 was sold for 20.
(h) Accounts receivable as at the end of 20X2 included 100 of interest receivable.
(i) Interest received during the year was 200 and dividends received during the year were 200. Payments on finance leases totaled 90.

Consolidated income Statement for the period ended 20 X 2	
Sales	30,650
Cost of sales	(26,000)
Gross profit	4,650
Depreciation	(450)
Administrative and selling expenses	(910)
Interest expense	(400)
Investment income	500
Foreign exchange loss	(40)
Profit before taxation	3,350
Taxes on income	(300)

	Profit	3,050

Consolidated Balance sheet as at end of 20 X 2

	20 X 2		20 X 1
Assets			
Cash and cash equivalents		230	160
Accounts receivable		1,900	1,200
Inventory		1,000	1,950
Portfolio investments		2,500	2,500
Property plant and equipment at coast	3,730		1,910
Accumulated depreciation	(1,450)		(1,060)
Property, plant and equipment net		2,280	
850			
Total assets		7,910	
6,660			
Liabilities			
Trade payables		250	
1,890			
Interest payable		230	
100			
Income taxes payable		400	
1,000			
Long-term debt		2,300	
1,040			
Total liabilities		3,180	
4,030			
Shareholder's Equity			
Share capital		1500	
1,250			

Retained earnings	3,230	
1,380		
Total shareholders' equity	4,730	
2,630		
Total liabilities and shareholders' equity	7,910	
6,660		

The cash flow statement now follows. Note that it is divided into two main parts:

- The cash flow statement itself
- Notes to the cash flow statement.

We have also added some working notes to help explain how the figures are arrived at.

Indirect Method Cash Flow Statement

	20
X 2	
Cash flows from operating activities	
Profit before taxation	3,350
Adjustments for:	
Depreciation	450
Foreign exchange loss	40
Investment income	(500)
Interest expense	400
	3,740
Increase in trade and other receivables	(500)
Decrease in inventories	1,050
Decrease in trade payables	(1,740)
Cash generated from operations	2,550
Interest paid	(270)
Income taxes paid	(900)
Net cash from operating activities	
1,380	
Cash flows from investment activities	
Acquisition of subsidiary X net of cash acquired (Note A)	(550)

149

Purchase of property, plant and equipment (Note B)	(350)
Proceeds from sale of equipment	20
Interest received	200
Dividends received	200
Net cash used in investing activities	
(480)	

Cash flows from financing activities

Proceeds from issue of share capital	250
Proceeds from long-term borrowings	250
Payment of finance lease liabilities	(90)
Dividends paid*	(1,200)

Net cash used in financing activities

(790)

Net increase in cash and cash equivalents

110

Cash and cash equivalents at beginning of period (Note C)

120

Cash and cash equivalents at end of period (Note C)

230

- This could also be shown as an operating cash flow

Note to the cash Flow statement

A: Acquisition of subsidiary

During the period, the Group acquired subsidiary X. the fair value of assets acquired

In addition, liabilities assumed as follows:

Cash	40
Inventories	100
Accounts receivables	100
Property, plant and equipment	650
Trade payables	(100)

Long-term debt	(200)
Total purchase price	590
Less Cash of X	(40)
Cash flow on acquisition net of cash acquired	550

B: Property, plant and equipment

During the period, the group acquired property, plant and equipment with an aggregate cost of 1,250 of which 900 was acquired by means of finance lease. Cash payments of 350 were made to purchase property, pant and equipment.

C: Cash and equivalents

Cash and equivalents consist of cash on hand and balance with banks, and investments in money instruments. Cash and equivalents included in the cash flow statement comprise the following balance sheet amounts:

	20 X 2	20 X 1
Cash on hand and balances with banks	40	25
Short-term investments	190	135
Cash and cash equivalents as previously reported	230	160
Effect of exchange rate changes	--	(40)
Cash and cash equivalents are restated	230	120

Cash and cash equivalents at the end of the period include deposits with banks of 100 held by a subsidiary with are not freely remissible to the holding company because of currency exchange restrictions.

The Group has undrawn borrowing facilities of 2,000 of which 700 may be used only for future expansion.

Further working notes

In arriving at the cash flow statement you will have had to make the following calculations and use the notes given in the additional information at the beginning of the exercise.

151

- Trade and other receivables:

Change on balance sheet for accounts receivable (1900-1200)	700
Deduct subsidiary receivables, as these will from part of the	
Acquisition under investing activities	100
Deduct Interest receivable as shown in investing activities	100
	500

- Inventories:

Change on balance sheet for inventory (1,000-1,950)	950	
Deduct subsidiary inventory acquired	100	
	1,050	

- Trade payables:

Change on balance sheet (250-1,890)	1,640
Deduct subsidiary trade payables	100
	1,740

- Interest paid is detailed in additional information note ©

- Taxation paid:

Opening balance of tax 9see note (e)	1,000
Tax provided in income statement	300
	1,300
Closing balance of tax	400
Therefore, cash paid in respect of tax	900

- Acquisition of subsidiary:

  Acquisition cost was 590 (note (a), but this included 40 cash, thus actual figure is 550

- Purchase of property, plant and equipment:

  This is actually provided at note (f), but we can calculate the figure from other information

  Given as follows:

Opening cost as per balance sheet	1,910
Add subsidiary assets acquired	650
	2,560

Add Finance lease (note (f))	900
	3,460
Deduct sale of plant (note (g))	80
	3,380
Closing cost as per balance sheet	3,730
Therefore, purchase	350

- Proceeds from sale of equipment is given in note (g)
- Interest received and dividends received are given in note (i)
- The proceeds from the issue of share capital and long term borrowings are given in note (b). the share capital can in fact be easily calculated from the balance sheet changes.
- Details of finance lease payments and dividends paid are given in notes (i) and (b) respectively.

As you can see from this exercise, to prepare a cash flow statement we need the provision of other information which is not shown in the income statement or the balance sheet.

Question for Practice

Now see if you can work the next example out for yourself.

The following information relates to peak Ltd:

Balance sheet as at 31 December 20 X 5

31.12.20 X 5

31.12.20 X 4

Property, plant and equipment nbv

Buildings	624,500		543,100
Other	102,300		93,450
Investments	142,000	868,800	56,000

692,550

Current assets:

Inventory	82,400		82,400
Debtors	48,750		54,300
Bank	_____		1,100
	132,150		137,800

Current liabilities falling due within one year:

Trade creditors	35,480		63,470
Taxation	12,500		10,500
Dividends	38,000		35,000
Bank	10,500		_____,
	96,480		108,970

Net current assets   35,670

28,830

Total assets less current liabilities   904,470

721,380

Non-current liabilities due after one year:

5% Debentures   150,000

45,000

154

Net assets	754,470	
676,380		
Capital reserves		
Ordinary £1 shares	620,000	
600,000		
Share premium account	40,000	
Revaluation reserve	70,000	
50,000		
Retained profits	24,470	
26,380		
	754,470	
676,380		

Income statement for the year ended 31 20X5

	20X5	20X4
	£	£
Profit before tax	48,590	65,600
Taxation	12,500	10,500
Profit after tax	36,090	55,100
Dividends	38,000	35,000
Retained profit for the year	(1,910)	20,100
Retained profit b/f 1 January	26,380	6,280
Retained profit at 31 December	24,470	26,380

The following additional information is available:

- A market issue of shares was made on 1 January 20X5.
- During 20X5, equipment originally purchased at £65,200 was sold for £17,900, accumulated depreciation being £37,700. The difference on disposal had been taken to the income statement.

155

- Buildings costing £100,000 had been purchased during 20X5 and the depreciation charged for the year 20X5 on other assets was £25,000. The only assets revalued during the year were the buildings.
- During 20X5, dividends received amounted to £7,500 and interest received £15,000, both of which had been credited to the income statement.
- The debentures were issued on 1 January 20X5 and interest due had been paid.

Required

(a) Prepare the cash flow statement for the year ended 31 December 20X5 in a form suitable for publication.

(b) Summarize the main conclusions arising from the cash flow produced for peak Ltd.

(c) Comment on the usefulness of the cash flow statement to users of financial statements.

Now check your answer with that provided at the end of the unit

FUNDS FLOW STATEMENTS.

As the cash flow statement highlights the change in cash and bank balance over the year, the **source and application of funds statement** highlights the **change in working capital** over the year. Working capital is current assets less current liabilities. The statement shows the sources of funds which have become available during the year, deducts the application of funds (i.e. how these funds have been applied during the year) and shows how the balance, i.e. net sources of funds, has been "ploughed into" inventories bank, etc.

Prior to the issue IAS 7, may entities included a statement of sources and application of funds in their published accounts. You may come across of funds flow statement, so it would be useful for you to understand its purpose.

Example

Source and Application of Funds Statement
For year ended 31 December

	£	£
Source of funds		
Profit before tax		47,000
Adjustment for items not involving the movement of funds:		
Depreciation		12,000
Funds generated from operations		59,000
Funds from other sources		
Issue of shares		15,000
		74,000
Application of Funds		
Purchase of non-current assets	6,000	
Payment of taxation	31,000	37,000
		37,000
Increase/Decrease in Working Capital		
Increase in inventory		21,000
Increase in trade receivables		2,000
Increase in trade payables		(2,000)
Movement in net liquid funds:		
Decrease in bank overdraft		16,000
		37,000

Reasons for change from Funds Flow

IAS7 set out to meet what the IAS identified as a move away in user needs from funds flow information to cash flow information (i.e. eliminating the long-term provisions and other allocations associated with accruals accounting). Reasons cited for the change in emphasis were:

1. Historical cash flows may be directly relevant for business valuation in a way that working capital flows are not.

2. Funds flow information may hide significant changes, through the leads and lags, as compared with cash flow, in the viability and liquidity of a business.

3. The funds flow statement does not provide any new data-it simply recognizes data already available in the balance sheet.

4. Cash flow is an easier concept to understand than working capital changes.

ANSWER TO QUESTION FOR PRACTICE

a. First we need to do the reconciliation of operating profit to net cash flow from operating activities:

	£	£
Net profit for the year before tax	48,590	
less interest and dividends received	22,500	26,090
add interest charged		7,500
Net profit before interest and tax		33,590
Depreciation on buildings	38,600	
Depreciation other	25,000	
Loss on sale	9,600	73,200
		106,790
Increase in inventory	(1,000)	
Decrease in debtors	5,550	
Decrease in creditors		(27,990)
(23,440)		
Net cash inflows from operating activities		
£83,350		

Now we can prepare the cash flow statement.

Cash Flow statement for Peak Ltd for the year ended 31.12.20X5

Net cash from operating activities		83,350
Interest paid	(7,500)	
Taxation paid	(10,500)	(18,000)
Net cash used in investing activities		
Payments to acquire tangible non-current assets	(161,350)	
Payments to acquire investments	(86,000)	
Sale of non-current assets	17,900	
Interest received	15,000	
Dividends received	7,500	(206,950)
Net cash used in financing activities		
Issue of shares	60,000	
Issue of debentures	105,000	
Equity dividends paid	(35,000)	130,000
Decrease in cash balances		£11,600

(a)   *The cash flow shows that:*

The amount generated from operating activities more than covered the net interest, dividends and tax paid for the company during the year ended 31 December 20X5.

Non-current assets were purchased in excess of sales of £229,450. This was financed by the issue of shares and debentures of £165,000 cash. The remaining £64,450 was financed from internal resources of the company resulting in cash reduction of £11,600.

The interest and dividends received on the investments is at a good level.

Questions should be asked in respect of the fall in the profit for the year.

Gearing has increased during the year, but does not appear to be at a high risk level.

The company has expanded its assets by the use of long-term capital resources in the main.

(C) *The cash flow statements are useful in that:*

It identifies the factors, which have caused the change in the cash and cash equivalent position.

It identifies the extent to which profits in inflows of cash.

It is more objective and verifiable than the income statement as it as no need for accruals and other estimated.

It provides information on something familial to users –cash. Users do not universally understand profit.

It provides information on the financial adaptability of a business and its liquidity. However, we could also say that.

The information provided is historical. Will this provide an indication of the future that can be relied on?

The format presentation, many would say, is disorganized and lacks clarity.

VALUATION OF INVESTORIES.

Accounting standards aim to narrow the differences and variations in practice and ensure adequate disclosure in published accounts. IAS 2 specifically seeks to define practices for the valuation of inventories.

To determine profit, costs have to be matched with related expenses. Unsold or unconsumed inventories and work in progress will have incurred costs in the expectation of future revenue and it is therefore appropriate to carry forward such costs so that they may be matched which future revenues.

The main requirement of IAS 2 is that **inventories** must be stated the **lower of cost or net realizable value-** this is the key point to remember.

Definitions.
(a) Inventories
Inventories are assets:
- Held for sale in the ordinary courses of business;
- In the process of production for such sale; and/or
- In the form of materials or supplies to be consumed in the production process or in the rendering of services.

Note that they do not include work –in progress arising under construction contacts.

These are dealt with under IAS 11 Construction contracts, which we will deal with later in this study unit.

(b) Cost
Cost is expenditure incurred in bringing the product or service to its present location and condition. There are elements to consider.

Cost of purchase
This comprises not just the purchase price of materials, etc, but any other costs incurred in acquiring them:
i. Purchase price
ii. Import duties
iii. Transport and handling costs and other attributable costs
iv. Trade discounts (subsidies and rebates must be deducted)

Trade discounts must not be confused with discounts which are allowed or received. **Cash discounts** are made to encourage the early payment of the account. **Trade discounts**, on the other hand, **never** appear in the books of accounts, and are deducted at source. The reason for these discounts:- if the seller will be dealing with three possible types of customer:

i. The trader who buys a lot
ii. The trader who buys only a few items
iii. The general public

It is therefore logical that whilst the three types of customer will want to benefit from a discount those under(i) will expect a higher discount that those under (ii) and those under (iii) a higher discount that those under (iv) This means that.

There would potentially be at least there price levels. To save staff having to deal with several price lists, all good are shown at the some price a negotiated trade of the transaction, are never therefore entered in the accounts.

Cost of conversion
The cost of conversion into finished goods consists of:
i. Cost attributable to units of production such as raw material, direct labor and expenses and sub-contracted work

ii.   Production overheads (see below)
iii.   Other overheads, if attributable in the particular circumstances of the business in bringing the product or service to its present location and condition.

Production overheads may cause some problems. The direct changes of raw materials, direct labor and expenses are easy to identify, but other overheads related to production may be difficult to define accurately, Fixed production overheads are those indirect costs of production that remain relatively constant regardless of the volume of production –for example, depreciation and maintenance of factory buildings. Variable production overheads are those indirect cost of production that vary directly, or nearly directly, with the volume of production such as indirect materials and indirect labor. The allocation of fixed production, overheads to the costs of conversion is based on the normal capacity of the production facilities. Variable production overheads are allocates to each unit of production on the basis of the actual use of he production facilities.

Where a production process results in more than one product being produced simultaneously, then costs of conversion are allocated between the products on a rational and consistent basis. For example, we coals base the allocation on the relative sales value of each product.

- Other cost.
Other costs are included in the cost of inventories only to the extent that they are incurred in bringing the inventories to their present location and condition. For example, we may need to include the costs of designing products for specific customers in the costs.

The standard specifically excludes several other costs:
i.   Abnormal amounts of wasted materials, labor or other costs
ii.   Storage costs, unless those costs are necessary in the production process before a further production stage –for example, maturing whisky or wine
iii.   Administrative overheads that do not contribute to bringing inventories to their present location and condition.
iv.   Selling costs.

Methods of Determining Cost.

If inventories are required to be measured at the lower of cost or net realizable value then we need firs to determine what the cost is. This is not always as was as it sounds.

(a) Unit Cost
This is the cost of purchasing or manufacturing identifiable units of inventory, and is the simplest form of determining cost. It can, though, be an impractical

method if the volume of inventories or the sales turnover is high. Thus, this method could be used for valuing luxury motor boats, but would be totally impractical for valuing tins of baked beans.

(b) Average Cost (Weighted Average)
The units of inventory on hand are multiplied by the average price. The average price is calculated by:

Total cost of units
Total number of units

(c) Simple average
The method is used to good advantage when it is impossible to identify each item separately, and the prices of purchases do not fluctuate very much. To calculate the issue price, the total **price** paid is divided by the **number of prices paid** in the calculation, for example:

| 1unit cost: | £1.00 per unit |
| 100 units cost: | £0.50 per unit |

Average price is $\frac{£ (1.00+0.50)}{2} = £0.75$

As you can see, a danger with this method arises where there are large variations in the numbers of items purchased.

(d) First In First Out (FIFO)
Here it is assumed that the earliest purchases are taken into production or sold first, and the inventory on hand then represents the latest production or purchases.

Advantages
The inventory valuation follows the physical movement of the inventory.

The most recent purchases appear on the balance sheet-as shown below.

Receipts Transaction		Issues	Inventory After Each	
Units	£	Units	£	Units £
20@ £ 45	£900		20 @ £45	

Receipts		Issues		Inventory After Each Transaction
10@ £50	£500			10 @ £50
£1,400				
		10 @ £45	£450	10 @£45
				10 @ £50
£950				
		10 @ £45		
		5 @ £50	£700	5 @ £50
£250				
10 @ £ 52	£520			5 @ £50
				10 @ £ 52
£770				

Disadvantages

The revenue is charged at current prices is potentially matched with out-of-date costs. This means that the profit is based on price change and the profit margin may not be consistent.

(e) Last In First Out (LIFO)

This works the opposite way to FIFO, and the calculation of inventories taken to production or sold represents the most recent purchases. Inventory on hand represents the earliest purchases or cost of production, as follows.

Receipts Transaction		Issues		Inventory After Each	
Units £	£	Units	£	Units	Units £
20@ £ 45	£900			20 @ £45	£
900					
10 @ £50	£500			20 @£45	
				10 @ £50	
£1,400					

	5 @ £50	£250	20 @ £45
£250			
			5 @ £50
£1,150			
10 @ £52 £520			20 @ £45
			5 @ £52
			10 @ £52
£1,670			
	5 @ £52	£260	20 @ £45
			5 @ £50
			5 @ £52
£1,410			

Advantages

The current revenue is matched with the current purchases, meaning that the profit should be realistic. In the ideal situation where items purchased equal items sold, the cost of sales will be the current cost of goods sold.

Disadvantages

The inventory values on the balance sheet are out-of-date and unrealistic. This is also the problem of keeping accurate records of inventory movements.

(f) Replacement Cost

This is the cost at which an identical asset could be purchased or manufactured. The difficult with this method arises where the replacement cost is greater than the historic cost because unrealized gains will be included in the resulting profit. Conversely, where the replacement cost is less than the reliable value or the historic cost, then a greater loss will be incurred.

Under IAS 2, LIFO method and replacement cost are not permitted for the valuation of inventories. Thus remember we can only use specific identification of costs, weighted average costs or FIFO.

Net Realizable Value

This is the actual or estimated selling price net of trade discounts, less:
- All further costs to completion
- All costs which will be incurred in marketing, selling and distribution.

Remember, the rule laid down in IAS 2 is that inventories must be valued at cost or net realizable value, whichever is the lower.

Estimates of net realizable value are based on the most reliable evidence available at the time the estimates are made. The writer down to net realizable value is charged to income statements as an expense.

There are many reasons why the net realizable value might be lower than cost:

- Errors in purchasing
- Errors in production
- Falling selling prices
- Obsolescence
- Increasing costs
- The company has decided to sell at a loss-for example, the supermarket practice of "loss leaders"

Balance sheet Disclosure of Inventories

Certain factors must be stated in the notes to published company accounts. The accounting policies used in calculating cost, net realizable value, attributable profit and foreseeable losses must all be stated.

Inventories should be analyzed in the balance sheet, or in notes to the financial statements, in a manner which is appropriate to the business, so as to indicate the amounts held in each of the main categories.

Remember that the amount at which inventories are valued in the final accounts directly affects the amount of gross profit.

Questions For practice.

1. This will help reinforce your understanding of manufacturing and trading accounts, as well as emphasizing the importance of the inventory figure (s).
   The trainee accountant in your costing department has tried to draw up a manufacturing and trading account as shown below.

   Required

   Correct the account.

	£	£
Opening inventories		20,590
Purchases	90,590	
Returns inwards	2,718	
	93,308	
less carriage inwards	4,920	
	88,388	
add Returns outwards	2,920	91,308
		111,898
add WIP 1 January		2,409
Prime cost		114,307
Indirect wages	10,240	
Direct expenses	9,110	
Factory insurance	2,240	21,590
		135,678
less WIP 31 Dec		5,219
		130,678
less Direct wages	14,209	
Indirect expenses	9,240	23,449
		107,229
add Finished goods 1 Jan		18,240
		125,469
less Finished goods 31 Dec		24,000
Cost of production		101,469
Sales		150,500
less Cost finished goods		101,469
		49,031
Add Closing inventories, 31 Dec		19,420
Trading profit		68,451

2. Calculate the cost of inventories in accordance with IAS 2 from be the following data relating to Mod enterprise for the year ended 31 December 200X.

$

Direct material cost of computer game per unit 2 Direct labour cost of

computer game per unit 2

168

Direct expenses cost of computer game per unit	2
Production overheads per year	500,000
Administrative overheads per year	300,000
Selling overheads per year	400,000
Interest payments per year	50,000

There were 150,000 units in finished goods at the year end. You may assume there were no finished goods at the start of the year and there was no work in progress. The normal level of production is 500,000 computer games, but in the year ended 31 December 200X only 350,000 was produced because of a labour dispute.

3. An entity has three products in its inventory with values as follows

Product	Cost	net Realizable Value
A	20	24
B	22	30
C	24	18
Total Inventory	66	72

At what value should the inventory be stated in the balance sheet in accordance with IAS 2?

Now check your answers with those provided at the end of the unit

A. VALUATION OF LONG-TERM CONTRACTS

Working in progress may include long-term contracts.

IAS 11: Construction contracts define a long-term contract as one that is undertaken to manufacture or build a single substantial entity, or to provide a substantial service. In both cases the period taken will extend **beyond one year,** and a substantial amount of the contract will be carried forward.

So what is the accounting problem with long-term contracts?

Well our problem is "how much of the revenue of the contract should we recognize in any one period?" A long term contract generally carries with it stage payments which may or may not relate to the stage of completion of the contract. Let's look at an example to demonstrate the problem.

Example

A construction contract with revenue of £20 m is initially estimated to have total of £12m and is expected to take three years to complete. Thus, over the life of the contract, there will be a profit of £8m, but at what point should we recognize that profit. If, for example, we receive stage payments of £5m in year 1, £5m in year 2 and £10m on final completion, should we recognize the profit as follows £2m in year 1, £2m in year 2 and £4m on completion-that is, in proportion to the stage payments?

If we reflect on some of the accounting concepts and conventions then we might be able to answer this question.

Reflecting the Fundamental Concepts

(a) Accruals Concept

The contract activity is expected to extend over several years, and it is argued that profit should be allocated over those years in order to give a "*true* and *fair view*" of the results of the years over which the activity takes place. A misleading view could be give if contract profits were not recognized until completion of the contract. Some years could show substantial profits and others substantial losses, causing the analyst to make incorrect interpretations on a company's progress.

(b) Prudence Concept

It may not be possible to predict accurately the outcome of a contract until the contract is well advanced. The prudence concept requires a company to determine the earliest point at which contract profit may be brought into the profit and loss account. Any contract has uncertainties, examples being the actual date on which the contract will be completed, or some unexpected cost arising. If it is expected that there will be a loss on any contract, provision should be made for a loss as soon as it becomes evident.

(c) Going Concern

A company entering into any contract must ensure that it has adequate resources to complete the contract.

(d) Consistency Concept

Where a company has several contracts of a similar nature, then it should treat such contracts in a similar fashion from an accounting point of view. In addition there should be consistency within any one year and from year to year.

IAS 11 Details

This is a difficult area of accounting and because of the wide variety of industrial projects there is, of course, a diversity of accounting practice. The IAS attempts to address this area by providing us with the following definitions and accounting practice.

Definitions

The IAS defines two types of contract;

- **A fixed price** contract is a construction contract in which the contractor agrees to a fixed price or a fixed rate per unit of output, which in some cases is subject to cost escalation clauses.
- **A cost plus** contract is a construction contract in which the contractor s reimbursed for allowable or otherwise defined costs, plus a percentage of these costs as a fixed fee.

The IAS does not define contract revenue for us, but it does tell us what it is comprised of. Contract revenue shall comprise.

- The initial amount of revenue agreed in the contract; and
- Variations in contract work, claims and incentive payments to the extent that it is probable that they will result in revenues, and are capable of being reliably measured.

Contract revenue needs to measure at its fair value.

The more difficult area in the standard is, of course, the recognition of contract costs to match with the revenue. There is no definition of contract costs, but the IAS states that contract costs comprise costs that relate directly to specific contracts, costs that are attributable to contract activity in general and can be allocated to the contract, and such other costs as are specifically chargeable to the customer under the terms of the contract.

Accounting practice

When the outcome of a construction contract can be estimated reliably then revenue and expense within the contract is recognized by reference to the stage of completion (and note that this is not necessarily the same as stage payments) of the contract. This is generally known as the percentage of completion method.

An expected loss on a long term contract must be recognized as an expense immediately in the income statement.

For debtors and creditors within long term contracts, the enterprise needs to disclose on its balance sheet:

- The gross amount due from customers (debtors) for contract work, which IAS 11 states is the net amount of costs incurred plus recognized profit less the sum of progress billings and recognized losses.
- The gross amount due to customers (creditors) is the net amount of costs incurred plus recognized profits less the sum of progress billings and recognized losses for all contracts in progress for which progress billings exceed costs incurred plus recognized profit.

All of the above may be somewhat confusion so again let us use an example to demonstrate accounting for long term contracts under the requirements of IAS 11.

Example

Show how the following information for two construction contracts should be recorded in the financial statements.

	Contract X	Contract Y
Contract revenue	500	350
Contract expenses	450	400
Billings	500	200
Payments in advance of billings	25	0
Contract costs incurred	600	400
Foreseeable additional losses	0	60

- For contract X

  Within the income statement, we will show revenue of 500 and expense of 450, resulting in a profit of 50. The difference between the contract costs incurred and contract expense (600-450 = 150) will be shown on the balance sheet under current assets as "due from customers, construction contract". In addition, the customer for this contract has paid us 25 in advance on billings. This will be shown on the balance sheet under "payments in advance, construction contracts".

- For contract Y

  This contract is only 10% complete4 and at this stage we are not able to reliably measure profit.

  Within the income statement, we will show contract revenue of 350 matched to contract costs of 400 plus the foreseeable loss (which must be recognized immediately) of 60, resulting in a loss of 110. Under "due from customers", we will need to show the 150-the difference between the contract revenue 350

172

billings 200-plus the provision for foreseeable loss of 60, so we have a net figure of 90 on the balance sheet under "due from customers, construction contracts".

In determining the point at which profit is to be recorded, the overriding principle is that there should be no attributable profit until the outcome of the contract can be foreseen with reasonable certainty. If the profit can be seen with reasonable accuracy it is only prudent that the profit earned should reflect the amount of work performance to date.

THE IMPORTANCE OF INVENTORY VALUATION

Closing inventory in Trading Account
Having reviewed the treatment of inventories in the manufacturing and trading accounts, we will now turn our attention to those organizations which do not have a manufacturing process. These firms will buy in finished goods for resale, and an example of a trading account is given below:

	£	£	£
Sales		25,770	
Less returns		1,446	24,324
Cost of good sold:			
Opening inventory		5,565	
Purchases	18,722		
Less returns	576		
	18,146		
Carriage inwards	645	18,791	
		24,356	
Less closing inventory		4,727	19,629
Gross (or trading) profit			4,695

After we have added purchases less returns to the opening inventory and added the carriage inwards, we have a grand total of the total inventory on hand plus all net purchases. From this figure we have to deduct the inventory remaining, i.e. unsold, because it is not part of the current year's costs. The net result is known as the **cost of sales**.

Unconsumed Inventories

The cost of unconsumed inventories will have been incurred in the expectation of future revenues which will not arise until a later period, and it is appropriate to carry this cost forward to be matched with the revenue when it does arise. This reflects the accruals concept-i.e. the matching of costs and revenue in the year in which they arise rather than in the year in which the cash is paid or received.

If there is no reasonable expectation of sufficient revenue to cover the cost incurred, the irrecoverable cost should be charged in the year under review. This may occur due to obsolescence, deterioration, change in demand, etc.

The comparison of cost versus realizable value needs to be made in respect of each item separately. Where this is not practical then groups or categories which are similar will need to be assessed together.

The methods used in allocating costs to inventory need to be selected with a view to providing the fairest possible assessment of the expenditure actually incurred in bringing the product to its present location and condition. For example in supermarkets and retail shops which have large numbers of rapidly changing items, it is appropriate to take the current selling price less group profit. When you next go shopping take a good look at the goods displayed and ask yourself how you think the retailer would go about valuing the inventory.

Inventories should be sub-classified so that the categories can be identified and this can be done in three ways:

- By maintaining detailed records of cost of sales
- By maintaining detailed records so that a inventory valuation may be performed at any time (known as the perpetual inventory)
- By using the gross profit margin applied to sales.

The inventories should also be classified and identified in the balance sheet or in notes to the accounts under the headings of:

- Raw materials
- Work in progress
- Finished goods

Gross or Trading Profit

As you know, the net sales less the cost of sales (sometimes known as the **cost of goods sold**) are the gross profit (GP). This is an important figure because it reveals the profit from operations.

Gross profit Ratio

This very simple calculation, and is usually quoted as a percentage:
$$\frac{\text{Gross profit}}{\text{Net sales}} \times 100$$

If we apply the figures from our trading account example above we get:

$$\frac{4,695}{24,324} \times 100 = 19\%$$

Most business has a target gross profit ratio which they aim to achieve. The success or failure of the business depends on maintaining a level of gross profit that will be higher than the expenses incurred in running the business. We will return to this subject in a later study unit when we discuss analysis of final accounts.

You should remember that the level of gross profit varies with the type of business. For example, the grocery trade, furniture stores and newsagents all have their individual profit margins, which may have vary even within the industry. A major supermarket chain may operate on quite different profit margins from that planned by a village store. However, it is generally possible to judge whether a business is below or above the average, once we are aware of the average gross profit for the particular trade. This will only be a rough guide because there are many other factors to take into account before a reasoned judgment can be made.

Stocktaking and Inventory Values
In large organizations inventory control systems usually exist and these adopt one of the methods we looked at earlier. In large supermarket and DIY stores, inventory will be computer-controlled from the tills, using scanning devices. Each sale not only records the value of the sale but also identifies the unit and updates the stock holding, often actually executing a re-order program automatically. This, of course, cuts out the arduous and expensive task of counting individuals of items inventory. Smaller firms, unable to afford sophisticated systems, do have to resort to counting the individual items.

The are various ways of doing this which range from the perpetual inventory to the once-a- year inventory check. Whichever method is chosen, there is the continual problem of pricing that stock. This is made easier by IAS 2 which suggests that it is acceptable to use the selling price less the estimated profit margin in the absence of a factory costing system. However, the chosen system must give a reasonable approximation of the actual cost.

Perpetual inventory

This a method of recording store balances after every receipt and issue to facilitate regular checking and to avoid the need to close down for stocktaking. The essential feature of the perpetual inventory is the continuous checking of stock. A number of items are counted every day or at frequent intervals and compared with stores records. Discrepancies can be investigated and clerical errors can be corrected. If there is a physical discrepancy, then the records must be adjusted accordingly. The usual causes of discrepancies are incorrect entries, breakage, pilfering, evaporation, short or over-issue, absorption by moisture, pricing method or simply putting the inventory in the wrong bin or location.

Effects of under-or over-Valuation of Inventory

The following three examples show the outcome if the closing inventory valuation is incorrect.

(a) Correct Inventory value

	£	£
Sales		10,000
Opening inventory	500	
Purchases	6,500	
	7,500	
Closing inventory	700	6,300
Gross profit		3,700

(b) Under-valuation

	£	£
Sales		10,000
Opening inventory	500	
Purchases	6,500	
	7,000	
Closing inventory	650	6,350
Gross profit		3,650

(c) Over-valuation

	£	£
Sales		10,000
Opening inventory	500	
Purchases	6,500	
	7,000	
Closing inventory	750	6,250
Gross profit		3,750

Notice the difference in the gross profit. These models show how important it is to get as accurate a inventory valuation as possible. Inventory adjustments are one of the main ways of "window dressing" a set of accounts, as well will see in a later study unit.

B. DEPRECIATION

Depreciation is a reduction in the value of an asset over a period of time. Fixed/non-current assets are those assets of a material value that are held for use in the business and not for resale or conversion into cash. With the exception of land, non- current assets do not last for ever and therefore have a limited number of years of useful life. In fact, even some land may have its usefulness exhausted after a number of years – examples include quarries, gravel pits and mines, but here it is possible that when one useful life is depleted, another useful life can be created. For example an old gravel pit can be filled with water and used for water sports.

Usually there is no one because that contributes to the reduction in value of an asset; it is more often a combination of factors. Externally there may be technological change and advancements causing obsolescence to existing assets, whilst internally there are inherent causes such as wear and tear in a factory environment.

Depreciation cannot really be determined accurately until the asset is disposed of .at that time the difference between the original cost and the disposal value can be matched. For accounting purposes it is unacceptable to wait the time of disposal, mainly because the total reduction in value would fall within one financial accounting period, whereas the reduction typically takes place over the whole of the period during which the asset is used.

Depreciation can be said to be that part of the cost of the cost of the asset which is consumed during its period of use by the firm. Depreciation is an expense and is treated in the some way as other expenses such as wages, electricity, rent, etc. However, the most significant underlying concept is that, unlike other charges in the income statement, the charge for depreciation does not entail actual expenditure.

Once the initial capital outlay has been made, no further amount is expended, although the firm is suffering a loss by reason of the diminution of the value of the asset which is retained in the business for the sole purpose of earning profit. This brings us back to the earlier rule that capital expenditure must not be mixed with revenue expenditure.

Accounting for Depreciation

The accounting entry is created by charging the relevant account, e.g. plant and machinery would be charged ion the manufacturing account unless there was no manufacturing account, in which case it would be charged in the profit and loss account. For delivery vehicles or salesmen's cars the charge would be shown in the distribution selection of the income statement.

If we choose a non-manufacturing firm as an example, then the entry in the income statement will be:

	£	£
Gross profit		29,250
Distribution expenses:		
Depreciation motor vehicles	1,000	
Administration expenses:		
Depreciation fixtures and fittings	2,000	3,000
		26,250

Balance sheet Disclosure

The following extract from a balance sheet shows how the asset and its related depreciation provision must be shown (these details may appear in notes to the final accounts):

	£	£
Non-current assets		
Fixture & fittings	9,000	
Less depreciation provision	2,000	7,000
Motor vehicles	11,000	
Less Depreciation provision	1,000	10,000

Remember the following two points:

- We must charge the accounts and at the same time create the provision as a credit balance.
- When it comes to the balance sheet, we match the asset and its relative provision.

Revaluation of Non-Current Assets

Where non-current assets are thought to have permanently increased in value, they may be included in the accounts at the revalued amounts. The depreciation charge is then calculated on the revalued amount. We will deal with a permanent decrease in the value, impairment, a little later in this study unit.

IAS 16 Property, plant and equipment Accounting for Depreciation

This section gives a summary of the requirements of IAS 16 in relation to depreciation in the published accounts of businesses.

Depreciation gives a summary systematic allocation of the depreciable amount of an asset over its useful life. Depreciable amount is the cost of an asset, or other amount substituted for cost, less its residual amount. Depreciation should be allocated to the accounting period so as to charge a fair proportion to each accounting period during the expected useful life of the asset.

It is important to remember that depreciation is just an accounting method for allocating the cost of an asset over the period of its use. The value of the asset in each intervening year has no real meaning, and it is certainly not what the asset could probably be sold at. The value is usually referred to as its **net book value**. Depreciation also has nothing to do with ensuring the business can afford to buy another asset when the first one becomes useless. Depreciation does NOT increase the amount of cash in a business. However, depreciation does have the effect of retaining resources by reducing profit and there by reducing potential dividend payments.

(a) Cost of an Asset
The cost of an asset is the amount of cash or cash equivalents paid, or the fair value of any other consideration given, to acquire an asset at the time of its acquisition or construction. The elements of this cost comprise;
- Its purchase price, including import duties and after deducting trade discounts and rebates.
- Any costs directly attributable to bringing the asset to the location and condition necessary for it to be capable o operating in the manner intended by management.
- The initial costs of dismantling and removing the item and restoring the site on which it is located the obligation for which an entity incurs at the time of acquisition.

Work through the following example to ensure you understand this definition of cost. In the year to 31 December 200X krang bought a new non-current asset and made the following payments in relation to it:

Cost as per supplier's list	24,000
Agreed discount	(2,000)
Delivery charge	200
Erection charge	400

Maintenance charge	600
Replacement parts	500
Estimated costs for restoring site at end of use	1,000

The cost will not include maintenance and replacement parts, which will be treated as on going expenses in relation to the asset, but the size restoration costs will be included.

Therefore, cost = 24,000 – 2,000 + 1,000 = 23,600

(b) Residual Value
This is the value which the firm could expect to recover at the end of the asset's useful life. It is a subjective matter and if there is any doubt then it should be treated as nil.

(c) Useful Life of an Asset
This is:
- Dependent upon the extent of use.
- Governed by extraction or consumption.
- Reduced by obsolescence or wear and tear.
- Predetermined as in leaseholds

This assessment is one the greatest problems since it depends upon the extent and pattern of future use. It can be described as the period over which the present owner will derive economic benefit from its use.

The assessment of depreciation considers three factors:

- The carrying amount of the assets, whether at cost or valuation
- The expected useful economic life
- The residual value.

The useful economic life should be reviewed regularly and, when necessary, revised such a review should normally be undertaken every five years and more frequently where circumstances warrant it.

(d) Methods of Depreciation
The IAS doe not lay down any specific methods but states that "there is a range of acceptable methods and management should choose the most appropriate to the asset and its use in the business". Management also need to review the depreciation method chosen at least each financial year and change the method

chosen if necessary. The new method will be applied to the net book value remaining in the books before the change.

It is not appropriate to omit a charge for depreciation.

Freehold land is not normally depreciated unless it is subject to depletion. However, the value of land may be adversely affected by considerations such as the desirability of its location, either socially or in relation to available sources of materials, labour, or sales and in such circumstances should be written down. All buildings have a finite life and should therefore be written down taking into consideration their useful economic life.

(e) Disclosures
The accounts should disclose the following information regarding each major class of depreciable asset:
- The method used
- The useful economic life or depreciation method used
- The total depreciation charged for the period.

(f) Revaluation of assets
Assets can be revalued if their fair value can be determined reliably.

If an item of property, plant and equipment is revalued, the entire class to which the asset belongs must be revalued. If an asset's carrying amount is increased under revaluation, then the increase is credited to a revaluation surplus, but if an asset's value is decreased then the entire fall in value is recognized in profit or loss, unless the fall reverses a previous valuation, in which case it can be debited to the remaining revaluation surplus.

Revalued assets must be still be depreciated, with the revalued amount now being treated as the cost determinant in the depreciation calculation.

(g) Changes in the method of Depreciation
Changes should only be undertaken if the new method gives a fairer presentation of the results and financial position.

(h) Scope of the standard
The standard applies to all non-current assets other than:
- Investment properties

- Goodwill
- Development costs
- Investments

C. METHODS OF PROVIDING FOR DEPRECIATION

Straight line method

The charge is calculated by taking the cost and deducting the residual value and dividing the result by the years of expected use. In some cases there may only be a scrap value if the asset has been used extensively in the business or if it is of a high-tech nature.

Suppose a motor vehicle was brought on the first day of the financial year for £10,000, the disposal or trade-in price was £1,000 and the expected period of usage was four years. If the vehicle is to be written off on a straight-line basis (i.e. equal amounts each year), then:

$$£10,000 - £1,000 = £9,000 \div 4 = \text{a charge of } £2,250 \text{ per annum}$$

The charge per annum is often expressed as a percentage of cost less residual value.

This is a very common method. It has the benefits that it is simple, effective and produces a uniform charge which affords better comparative costs. The straight-line method is ideal for assets such as lease, copyrights, etc. although it is also commonly used for plant and machinery and motor vehicles.

The argument against the method is that an equal amount is charged each year, even through maintenance charges may be low in the early years of the asset's use and rise in the later years.

Reducing Balance method

This is also sometimes known as the **fixed percentage method** because a percentage is determined and applied each year to the **reducing balance** of the capital value.

Say we have an asset worth £12,000 with residual value of £2,000 and choose a rate of 50%. In Year 1 the charge will be £5,000, but in the following year the charge will be calculated on the reduced capital value of £5,000 and so would be £2,500-the year after, the charge would be £1,250 and so on. Those who favor this method claim that the high charge in the earlier years offsets lower maintenance costs, and in the later years the higher maintenance costs are offset by the reduced depreciation charge.

You should also note that this method never writes off the asset completely.

Sum of the Years Digits.

This is not as popular a method in Britain as it is in the USA. It follows the same principle as the reducing balance method but it is easier to use because there is no difficult computation when assessing the amount to be charged.

Again, if we buy an asset for £10,000 with a life of four years and the residual value is estimated to be £2,000, we would write down the asset over four years by weighting earlier years' charges higher than later years. Therefore over four years the charge in year 1 would be assigned a value of 4, in year 2 a value of 3, in year 3 a value of 2, and year 4 a value of 1, as follows:

2 + 3 + 2 +1 = 10 or 4 (4 + 1) ÷ 2 10

For example:

Year 1: 4/10ths x £8,000 = 3,200

Year 2: 3/10ths x £8,000 = 2,400

Year 4: 1/10ths x £8,000 =   800 = £8,000 total

D. BOROWING COSTS AND IAS 23

Previously in this study unit we discussed the cost of an asset. Within that cost, we did not consider whether borrowing costs, interest incurred on loans, etc. used to acquire the asset, formed part of that cost. Remember the cost of an asset is all those expenses required to enable the asset to be brought into use. Could we then make a case for considering the interest on any loan needed as part of that cost?

In the case of a self-constructed asset, where we can directly allocate the borrowing costs, these can be logically regarded as part of the cost. But it is not always clear which loan applies to which asset, so should these interest/borrowing costs be regarded as part of the cost or not? Clearly, if we don't capitalize the borrowing costs as part of the cost of an asset, then they will need to be expensed to the income statement. Expensing all such borrowing costs would clearly be prudent.

These issues are considered by IAS 23 which, in its most recent form, was issued in 1994 and minor changes made to it in March 2007.

Accounting Treatment

This standard states that borrowing costs shall be recognized as an expense in the period in the period in which they are incurred. That is very clear. However, the standard goes on to sate "except to the extent that they are capitalized". Thus, the standard permits us to capitalize some borrowing costs. But which? The answer is "borrowing costs that are directly attributable to the acquisition, construction or production of a qualifying asset shall be capitalized as part of the cost of that asset".

- A qualifying asset for the capitalization of borrowing costs is one that necessarily takes a substantial period of time to get ready for its intended use or sale.
- Borrowing costs are defined as those that could be avoided if the asset had not been acquired.

It can be quite difficult to identify a direct relationship between an asset and borrowing costs, especially if funds are borrowed generally and controlled by a central function within the business. In these cases, the standard permits us to apply a capitalization rate to the expenditure on the asset. This rate is a weighted average.

E. LEASED ASSETS AND IAS 17

A lease is an agreement that conveys to one part, the lessee, the right to use property, but does not convey legal ownership of that property. However, the IASB's Framework does not define an asset in relation to legal ownership. Remember an asset is a resource controlled by an entity as a result of a past event and from which future economic benefits are expected to flow to the entity. So, can a leased asset be viewed as an asset of the lease and not that of the lesser? If it is viewed as an asset of the lease, then this will make a considerable difference to the balance sheet of the business as the will have to be capitalized at its fair value and then depreciated. In additional, the amount owed to the lesser under the lease agreement will need to b shown as liability.

Classification of leases

The standard divides leases into finance leases and operating leases. Finance leased assets are those that we will need to capitalize on to the balance sheet of the leases as they fit the description of an asset.

- A finance lease is a lease that transfers substantially all the risks and rewards incidental to ownership of an asset. Title may or may not eventually be transferred.
- An operating lease is a lease other than a finance lease.

Accounting Treatment

IAS 17 requires us to recognize a finance lease in the lease's balance sheet at amounts equal to the fair value of the leased property or, if lower, the present value of the minimum lease payments determined at the inception of the lease.

A finance lease will also give rise to depreciation expenses over the useful life of the leased asset. However, be a little careful here as the useful life of a leased asset is only the remaining period from the commencement of the lease over which the economic benefits embodied in the leased asset are expected to be consumed by the lease.

The interest payable on the lease needs to be allocated to accounting periods during the lease so as to produce a constant periodic rate of charge on the remaining balance of the obligation for each accounting period.

Examples

We can best demonstrate the classification and accounting for leases by the use of the following examples.

Example 1

X business acquires four identical pieces of equipment on the same day as follows:

- Piece 1, rented from A at a cost of £500 per month payable in advance and terminable at any time by either party.
- Piece 2, rented from B at a cost of eight half-yearly payments in advance of £3,000
- Piece 3, rented from C at a cost of six half-yearly payments in advance of £2,400
- Piece 4, purchased outright from D at a cost of £16,000

Which of the above are non-current assets of X?

Obviously, piece 4 is a non-current asset of X as this is a purchased asset. The purchase price also sets the fair value of the piece of equipment-£16,000.

Piece 1 is an operating lease as there is no transfer of the risks and rewards to X.

Piece 2 involves a total payment asset of £24,000 which in present value terms will be more than the fair value. Therefore, this is a finance lease and 2 is a non-current asset of X.

Piece 3 only involves a total payment of £14,400, the present value of which will be significantly less than £16,000 and this, therefore, is an operating lease.

Example 2.

A lessee leases an asset for a period of five years. The rental is £650 per quarter payable in advance. The leased asset could have been purchased for £10,000 and has a useful life of 8 years. Show how the lease will be accounted for in the lessees' books for the first year. The rate of interest implicit in the lease, the constant periodic charge, is 2.95% per quarter.

In this example, the lease is a finance lease as total payments are £ 13.000, which in present value terms is more than. £ 10,000. At the beginning of the lease period, the asset will be capitalized in the lease's books by debiting non-current assets £ 10,000 and crediting liabilities loans £ 10,000.

The lease payments total £ 13,000 and, therefore, the total interest charge in the lease is £ 3,000. This interest has to be allocated across the reducing balance of liability as follows:

Period	Capital sum at start	Rental paid	Capital sum during period	Finance charge 2.95%	Capital sum at end
1	10,000	650	9350	276	9626
2	9626	650	8976	265	9241
3	9241	650	8591	254	8845
4	8845	650	8195	<u>242</u>	8437

				1,037	
8437	8437	650	7787	230	8017
8017	8017	650	7367	217	7584
7584	7584	650	6934	205	7139
7139	7139	650	6489	<u>191</u>	668 0
				<u>843</u>	

The annual lease charge of 4 x 650 = £2,600 can now be allocated to capital repayment and expense interest charge. In the first year, the interest charge is 1,037 and therefore capital repayment is 1,563. In the second year, the capital repayment due will be 1,757 (2,600 – 843).

Thus, in the financial statements for year 1, the income statement will be charged with 1,037 interests and the liability will be reduced by 1,563. Of the remaining liability of 8,437, the next yearly capital repayment will be recognized as a current liability 1,757.

We also need to deprecate the asset. It value is 10,000 and we shall assume no residual value and that the useful life will be five years as this is the lesser of the lease period and the useful life of the asset – in other words, the useful life to the lessee is curtailed by the length of the lease period. Depreciation charge will, therefore, be 2, 000 per annum.

F. IAS 36: IMPAIRMENT OF ASSETS

The essential objective of IAS 36 is to ensure that all assets are no5t carried at a figure greater than their recoverable amount. Is essential requirement is that when an asset is impaired – that is, its recoverable amount becomes less than its carrying amount in the books – this loss must be written off.

IAS 36 is applicable to all assets except inventories (see IAS 2), construction contracts (see IAS 11), deferred tax assets (see IAS 12), employee benefits, insurance contracts, investment properties (see section I which follows and IAS 40), and assets held for sale in accordance with IFRS 5. This means IAS 36 also applies to intangible assets such as goodwill. Impairment reviews are also required on those assets that have previously been revalued upwards.

Requirements of IAS 36

IAS 36 requires that, at each balance sheet date, an assessment must be carried out to determine whiter their are any indications of impairment of assets. If there are indications of impairment, then the business needs to estimate the recoverable amount of the asset and compare this with the carrying amount.

IAS 36 suggests the following as indications of impairment:

- An asset's market value has decided significantly more than would be expected as a result of the passage of time \or normal use.
- Significant changes with an adverse effect on the business have taken place or will take place in the technological, market, economic or legal environment in which the business operates.
- Market interest rates have increased during the period and those increase are likely to affect the discount rate used in calculating asset's value in use and decrease the asset's recoverable amount materially.
- The carrying amount of the net assets of the business is more than its market capitalization.

Example

Again let us use an example to demonstrate the requirements of the standard.

A non-current asset was purchased for £2m several years ago and revalued after 5 years to £3m. at this stage, a revaluation reserve of £1m was created. In the current year, an impairment review is undertaken and the recoverable amount of the asset is found to be £1.2m. The impairment incurred is, therefore, £1.8m. £1m of this impairment will be charged to the revaluation reserve and £0.8m to the income statement.

G. IAS 40: INVESTMENT PROPERTIES

IAS 1 defines a non-current asset as any asset other than a current asset. Current assets are defined by IAS 1 as an asset which is:

- Expected to be realized, or intended for sale or on consumption, in the business's normal operating cycle.
- Held primarily for the purpose of being traded.
- Expected to be realigned with 12 months
- Cash or cash equivalent.

This is all well and good, but what about a business which owns property which it intends to hire out in the short to medium term and eventually sell. Is this a current asset or non-current asset?

The answer seems to depend on the particular operating activities of the business. If the business is actually trading in properties as an operating activity, then the property would seem to be a current asset. If the business is intending to hold the property for a number of accounting periods, then perhaps non-current denomination better reflects the substance. However, the property is still not being consumed in supporting the operating activities of the business, presuming it is not trading in property, and therefore charging depreciation on the asset would seem to be incorrect.

IAS 40 provides the following definition:

- An investment property is a property (land and/or building) held to earn rentals or for capital appreciation rather than for use in the production or supply of goods or sale in the ordinary course of business.

Investment properties are recognized as a non-current asset in the financial statements at cost or fair value. If a business opts for the fair value model, then changes in fair value from one period to the next will be recognized in the income statement. If a cost model is chosen, then IAS 16 comes into force and the property is depreciated.

Note that choosing the fair value method for an investment property which is increasing in value will enhance the profit declared by a company as the gain is taken to the income statement, where as under the cost model, the profit declared would be reduced due to depreciation. This something for you to be aware of when analyzing financial statements.

(Also be aware that IAS 40 is very different to the UK SSAP 19 where a fair value method is enforced and increases in fair value are taken to an investment property reserve).

The decision tree below is useful in applying IAS 40.

Figure 6.1: Decision tree for treatment of most property under IAS GAAP

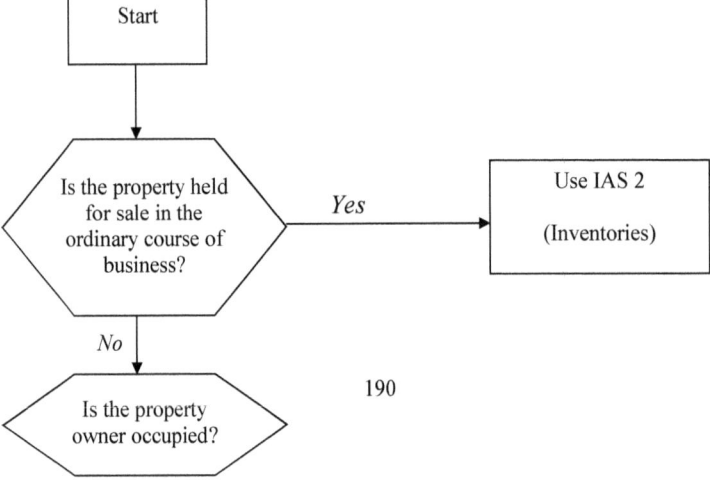

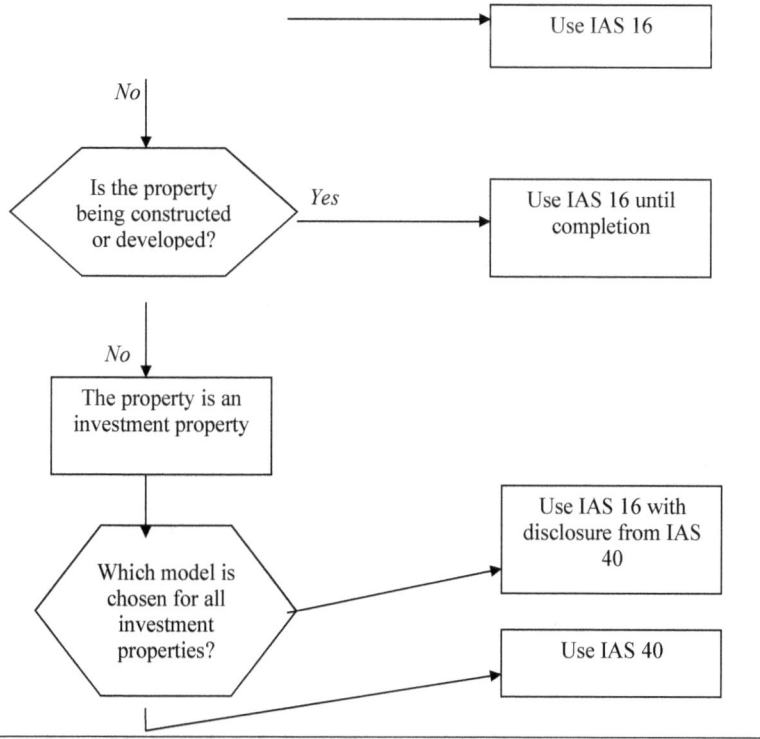

Questions for practice

4. J limited purchased the following assets on 1 January: building at £150,000, plant and machinery at £75,000, fixtures and fittings at £50,000 and motor vehicles at £35,000. The company's financial year ends on 31 December.

    Calculate the depreciation using the straight-line method.

    The percentage rates of depreciation to be applied are: buildings 2% pa, plant and machinery 25% pa, fixture and fittings 2 ½ % pa, and motor vehicles 25% pa.

    It is assumed that the residual values will be as follows: buildings nil, plant £2,000, fixtures £8,000 and motor vehicles £5,000.

5. Calculate the depreciation on the following assets, showing exactly how much will be charged annually in respect of each. Use the sum of the year's digits methods.

(a) Plant costing £150,000 with a residual value of £10,000 and an expected useful life of 5 years.

(b) Fixtures and fittings costing £25,000 with a residual value of £1,000 and an expected life of 15 years.

(c) Motor vehicles costing £45,000 with a residual value of £5,000 and an expected life of 4 years.

6. Consider each of the assets described below and indicate whether or not they are investment properties as defined in IAS 40.

(a) Land held for long term capital appreciation rather than for short term sale in the ordinary course of business.

(b) Land held for a currently undetermined use.

(c) Property that is being constructed or developed for future use as investment property.

(d) A building owned by a business and leased out under operating leases

(e) A building that is vacant, but is held for operating lease purchases.

(f) Property intended for sale in the ordinary course of business.

(g) Property being constructed for third parties.

(h) Owner occupied property

(i) Property leased to others under a finance lease

Now check your answers with those provided at the end of the unit.

ANSWER TO QUESTIONS FOR PRACTICE

1. The corrected account is as follows:

Manufacturing and Trading Account

	£	£
Opening inventories		20,590
Purchases	90,590	
less carriage inwards	4,920	
	95,510	
Returns outwards	2,920	92,590

		113,180
Closing inventories		19,420
		93,760
Direct wages	14,209	
Direct expenses	9,110	23,319
Prime cost		117,079
Indirect wages	10,240	
Indirect expenses	9,240	
Factory insurance	2,240	21,720
		138,799
add WIP 1 Jan		2,409
		141,208
less WIP 31 Dec		5,219
Cost of production		135,989
Sales	150,500	
less Return	2,718	147,782
Opening inventories	18,240	
Cost of production	135,989	
	154,229	
Closing inventories (finished goods)	24,000	130,229
Gross trading profit		17,553

2. The direct costs of the computer game are simple enough to calculate as follows:

150,000 units at $2 material cost	300,000
150,000 units at $2 labour costs	300,000
150,000 units at $2 expenses costs	300,000
	900,000

IAS 2 only permits the inclusion of overhead cost in the valuation of inventories and, therefore, administration, selling's and interest cannot be included. If we assume the production overheads are fixed in nature, then we must allocated these based on normal production capacity which, in this case, is 500,000 units.

$$production\ overheads = \frac{500,000}{500,000}x150,000 \qquad \underline{150,000}$$

Cost of finished inventories   <u>1,050,000</u>

The abnormal costs associated with the labour dispute will be charged as an expense in the period in which they incurred.

3. IAS e requires us to each type of inventory separately. So the answer is not 66, the lower of total cost or net realizable value.

    The answer is 20 + 22 + 18 = 60

4.

Depreciation Asset	Cost £	Residual Value £	Depreciate On £	£
Buildings	150,000	Nill	150,000	3,000
Plant	75,000	2,000	73,000	18,250
Fixtures & fittings	50,000	8,000	42,000	5,250
Motor vehicle	35,000	5,000	30,000	7,500

5.

Year Motor Vehicle	Plant £	Year	Fixtures And fitting £	Year	£
1 16,000	46,666	1	3,000	1	

2	37,333	2	2,800	2
12,000				
3	27,999	3	2,600	3
8,000				
4	18,666	4	2,400	4
4,000				
5	9,336	5	2,200	
40,000				
	140,000	6	2,000	
		7	1,180	
		8	1,600	
		9	1,400	
		10	1,200	
		11	1,000	
		12	800	
		13	600	
		14	400	
		15	200	
			24,000	

6. (a), (d) and (e) are clearly investment properties.

(b) Is speculative at the moment, but would be regarded as an investment property at this stage.

www.ingramcontent.com/pod-product-compliance
Lightning Source LLC
Chambersburg PA
CBHW051649170526
45167CB00001B/397